GARDENING INDOORS AND UNDER GLASS

A Practical Guide to the Planting, Care and Propagation of House Plants, and to the Construction and Management of Hotbed, Coldframe and Small Greenhouse.

by
F. F. Rockwell

FOREWORD

There is nothing which adds so much sunshine and cheer to the rooms of a house besieged by winter and all his dreary encampment of snow and ice, as the greenery, color and fragrance of blossoming plants. There is no pastime quite so full of pleasure and constant interest as this sort of horticulture; the rooting of small slips, the repotting and watering and watching, as new growth develops, and buds unfold. Some have the magic gift, that everything they touch will break into blossom; others strive — perhaps too hard — only to gain indifferent results. It is hoped that this book will aid those of the second class to locate past mistakes and progress to future success; and further that it may indicate to those more fortunate ones of the first class the way to more extensive achievements in the work they love.

This is not a technical book; simply an attempt to tell in so plain a way that they cannot be misunderstood the everyday details of the successful management of plants in the house and within such small glass structures as may be made, even with limited means and time, a part of the average home.

There is another aspect of the case worth considering; so much so in fact, that it is one of the reasons for writing this book. By the use of such modest glass structures as almost everyone can afford not only is the scope of winter gardening enlarged and the work rendered more easy and certain, but the opportunity is given to make this light labor pay for itself. Fresh vegetables out of season are always acceptable and well grown plants find a ready sale among one's flower-loving friends.

CRANMERE, August 1st, 1912.

F. F. R.

CONTENTS

PART I—PLANTS IN THE HOUSE

CHAPTER		PAGE
I	INTRODUCTION	1
II	THE PROPER CONDITIONS: LIGHT, TEMPERATURE AND MOISTURE	6
III	SOILS, MANURES AND FERTILIZERS	14
IV	STARTING PLANTS FROM SEED	22
V	STARTING PLANTS FROM CUTTINGS	29
VI	TRANSPLANTING, POTTING AND REPOTTING	35
VII	MANAGEMENT OF HOUSE PLANTS	44
VIII	FLOWERING PLANTS	51
IX	SHRUBS	70
X	FOLIAGE PLANTS	81
XI	VINES	90
XII	FERNS	97
XIII	PALMS	103
XIV	CACTI	110
XV	BULBS	116
XVI	VERANDA BOXES, WINDOW-BOXES, VASES AND HANGING BASKETS	128
XVII	HOUSE PLANT INSECTS AND DISEASES	132
XVIII	ACCESSORIES	140

PART II—HOME GLASS

XIX	ITS OPPORTUNITIES	146
XX	THE COLDFRAME AND THE HOTBED	149

CONTENTS

CHAPTER   PAGE

XXI   THE CONSTRUCTION OF CONSERVATORIES AND SMALL GREENHOUSES 156

XXII   METHODS OF HEATING 167

XXIII   MANAGEMENT 172

XXIV   FLOWERS 180

XXV   VEGETABLES 193

XXVI   VEGETABLE AND BEDDING PLANTS FOR SPRING 197

INDEX 207

ILLUSTRATIONS

A flourishing flower bay . . . . *Frontispiece*

FACING PAGE

An isolated bay-window conservatory 8
A tiled window-sill garden 9
Preparing flats for the "sub-irrigation" method of water-
    ing 28
Cuttings ready for sand 29
Geranium cuttings ready for potting 29
Potted cuttings ready for their first shift 40
Striking Rex begonia leaf cuttings 40
"Crocking" in a flower pot 41
Seedlings ready to transplant 48
A flower bay protected with heavy curtains 49
Pride of Cincinnati begonia 60
Pansy geranium 61
Primrose (*Primula obconica*) 61
The Silk Oak (*Grevillea robusta*) 72
Otaheite orange 73
Baby rambler rose 80
Araucaria excelsa 81
Screw Pine (*Pandanus Veitchii*) 88
Rubber plant (*Ficus elastica*) 89
Vines on an indoor trellis 96
Crested Scott Fern (*Nephrolepis exaltata*, var. *Scholzeli*) 97
Propagation of Boston Fern by division 100
A variety of the Fan Palm (*Phoenix Roebelenii*) . . 101
Weddell's Palm 101
A pan of forced crocuses 116
Victory gladiolus 117
A second story window-box 128
Iceland poppies and trailing vines in a window-box . . 128
A movable plant table 129
Inside a small greenhouse 148
A small lean-to greenhouse 149
A three-sash coldframe 164
The simplest type of window greenhouse 165
Tomatoes in the greenhouse 196
Cucumbers and lettuce in the greenhouse 197

GARDENING
INDOORS
AND UNDER GLASS

Part One—Plants in the House

CHAPTER I

INTRODUCTION

TO-DAY the garden is in the zenith of its glory. The geraniums and salvias blaze in the autumn sun; the begonias have grown to a small forest of beautiful foliage and bloom; the heliotropes have become almost little trees, and load the air with their delicate fragrance. To-night — who knows? — grim winter may fling the first fleet-winged detachment of his advance across the land, by every road-side and into every garden-close; and to-morrow there will be but blackening ruins and burned bivouacs where the thousand camps of summer planted their green and purple in the golden haze.

And what provision, when that inevitable day of summer's defeat comes, have you made for saving part of the beauty and joy of your garden, of carrying some rescued plants into the safe stronghold of your house, like minstrels to make merry and cheer the clouded days until the long siege is over, and spring, rejuvenescent, comes to rout the snows?

I do not know which is the more commonly overlooked, the importance and fun of keeping the living-rooms of the house cheerful with plants and flowers in winter, or the certainty and economy with which it may be done if one will use the plain common-sense methods necessary to make plants succeed. Too much care and coddling is just as sure to make growth forlorn and sickly as too much neglect. That may be one reason why one frequently sees such healthy looking plants framed in the dismal window of a factory tenement, where the chinks can never be stopped tight and the occupants find it hard enough to keep warm, while at the same time it is easy to find leafless and lanky specimens in the super-heated and moistureless air of drawing-rooms.

It certainly is true that many modern houses of the better sort do not offer very congenial conditions to the healthy growth of plants. It is equally certain that in many cases these conditions may be changed by different management in such way that they would be not only more healthy for plants to live in, but so also for their human occupants. In many other cases there is nothing but lack of information or energy in the way of constructing a place entirely suitable for the growth of plants. To illustrate what I mean, I mention the following instance of how one person made a suitable place in which to grow flowers. Two narrow storm windows, which had been discarded, were fastened at right angles to the sides of the dining-room windows, and the regular storm sash screwed on to these. Here were the three glass sides of a small conservatory. Half-inch boards made a bottom and roof, the former being supported by brackets to give strength, and the latter put on with two slanting side pieces nailed to the top of the upright narrow sash spoken of, to give the roof a pitch. Top and bottom were covered with old flexible rubber matting which was carried back under the clapboards making a weather-proof, tight joint with the side of the house. Six-inch light wooden shelves on the inside gave a conservatory of considerable capacity. How many houses there are where some such arrangement could be made as the result of a few hours' work and thought, and a very small expense. And yet how infrequently one sees anything of the kind. In many instances such a glassed-in window would be all that is needed, sufficient heat being furnished by a radiator under the window within the house. In the case mentioned, however, it was necessary to heat the small greenhouse. This was done by installing a small gas stove in the cellar, as nearly as possible under the window greenhouse. Over this stove a large tin hood was fitted, with a sliding door in front to facilitate lighting and regulating the stove. From the hood a six-inch pipe, enclosed in a wood casing for insulation, ran through the cellar window and up into the floor of the conservatory, ending in a small radiator.

These details are given not with the idea that they can be duplicated exactly (although in many instances they might), but to show what a little ingenuity and effort will accomplish in the way of overcoming difficulties.

Nor is the reward for such efforts as these restricted to the growing of a few more plants. From the actual accomplishments described in the second part of this book, the reader must see that it is entirely possible and feasible for one with only average advantages to have during a large part or even all of the year not only flowers which cannot be grown to advantage in the house, but also such vegetables as lettuce, radishes, tomatoes and cucumbers, and others if desired; and also to give the flower and vegetable gardens such a start as would never be possible otherwise.

Do not attempt too much, but do not be content with too little, when only a slight increase in planning and work will bring such a tremendous increase in results and happiness. I feel confident that there is not one home out of ten where more thought and more information brought to bear on the things whereof this book treats, would not yield a greater return in actual pleasure than any other equal investment which could be made.

Do not be impatient to get to a description of all

the results at once. Do not skip over the chapters
on dirt and manures and pots and other seemingly
uninteresting things, because in a thorough under-
standing of these essentials lies the foundation of
success. And if a condition of soil, or an operation
in handling plants does does not seem clear to you
as you read it over, remember that in all probability
it will become so when you actually attempt the
work described. Nothing worth while is ever won
without a little — and often a great deal — of
patient work. And what is more worth while than
to keep busy in the constant improvement and
beautifying of one's daily surroundings?

CHAPTER II

THE PROPER CONDITIONS: — LIGHT, TEMPERATURE AND MOISTURE

AFTER so much advice as to the possibility of making conditions right for the growing of plants in the house, the inexperienced reader will naturally want to know what these conditions are.

LIGHT

In the first place, almost all plants, whether they flower or not, must have an abundance of light, and many require sunshine, especially during the dull days of winter. Plants without sufficient light never make a normal, healthy growth; the stems are long, lanky and weak, the foliage has a semi-transparent, washed-out look, and the whole plant falls an easy victim to disease or insect enemies. Even plants grown in the full light of a window, as everyone with any experience in managing them knows from observation, will draw toward the glass and become one-sided with the leaves all facing one way. Therefore even with the best of conditions, it is necessary to turn them half about every few days, preferably every time they are watered, in order that they may maintain an even, shapely growth.

As a rule the flowering plants, such as geraniums and heliotropes, require more light and sunshine than those grown for foliage, such as palms, ferns and the decorative leaved begonias. It is almost impossible, during the winter months, to give any of them too much sunlight and where there is any danger of this, as sometimes happens in early fall or late spring, a curtain of the thinnest material will give them ample protection, the necessity being not to exclude the light, but simply to break the direct action of the sun's rays through glass.

A great variety of plants may be grown in the ordinary window garden, for which the sunniest and broadest window available should be selected. There are two methods of handling the plants: they may be kept as individual specimens in pots and "dishes" or "pans" (which are nothing more or less than shallow flower pots), or they may be grown together in a plant box, made for the purpose and usually more or less decorative in itself, that will harmonize with and set off the beauty of the plants.

The latter method, that of growing in boxes, offers two distinct advantages, especially where there is likely to be encountered too high a temperature and consequent dryness in the air. The plants are more easily cared for than they are in pots, which rapidly dry out and need frequent changing; and effects in grouping and harmonious decoration may be had which are not readily secured with plants in pots. On the other hand, it is not possible to give such careful attention to individual plants which may require it as when they are grown in pots; nor can there be so much re-arrangement and change when these are required — and what good house-keeper is not a natural born scene shifter, every once in so often rolling the piano around to the other side of the room, and moving the bookcase or changing the big Boston fern over to the other window, so it can be seen from the dining-room?

If the plants are to be kept in pots — and on the whole this will generally be the more satisfactory method — several shelves of light, smooth wood of a convenient width (six to twelve inches) should be firmly placed, by means of the common iron brackets, in each window to be used. It will help, both in keeping the pots in place and in preventing muddy water from dripping down to the floor or table below, if a thin, narrow strip of wood is nailed to each edge of these shelves, extending an inch or two above them. A couple of coats of out-side paint will also add to the looks and to the life of these shelves and further tend to prevent any an-noying drip from draining pots. Such a shelf will be still further improved by being covered an inch or two deep with coarse gravel or fine pebbles.

If possible it is well to have the house plants in a place
where the moisture and temperature can be regulated for
them alone

In almost any house it is possible to arrange a wide sill with a metal or tile bottom where house plants may be properly cared for

This is much better than the use of pot saucers, especially for small pots. Where a bay-window is used, if cut off from the room by glass doors, or even by curtains, it will aid greatly in keeping a moist atmosphere about the plants and preventing dust from settling on the leaves when sweeping or dusting is being done.

A window-box can readily be made of planed inch pine boards, tightly fitted and tightly joined. It should be six to ten inches wide and six to eight inches deep. If a plain box is used, it will be necessary to bore inch holes every six inches or so through the bottom to provide for carrying off of any excess of water — although, with the method of filling the box described in a later chapter, those holes would hardly ever be called into service. Plants in the house in the winter, however, are as likely to suffer from too much water as from too little, and therefore, to prevent the disagreeable possibility of having dirty drainage water running down onto several feet of floor, it will be almost as easy, and far better, to have the box constructed with a bottom made of two pieces, sloping slightly to the center where one hole is made in which a cork can be kept. A false bottom of tin or zinc, with the requisite number of holes cut out, and supported by three or four inch strips of wood running lengthways of the box, supplies the drainage. These strips must, of course, be cut in the

middle to allow all the water to drain out. The
false bottom will take care of any ordinary surplus
of water, which can be drained off into a watering
can or pitcher by taking out the cork. The details of construction of such a box are shown in
figure 1. It will be best to have the box so placed

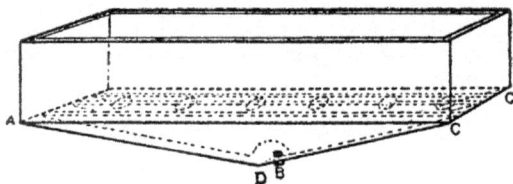

Fig. 1—Box for plants. AC—false zinc bottom;
AB, CB—slanting bottom to drain water out at
hole B.

upon its supporting brackets that it can be changed
occasionally end for end, thus keeping the plants
growing evenly, and not permitting the blooms con-
tinually to turn their backs to the inside of the
room.

With the above simple provisions one may take
advantage of all the light to be had in an ordinary
window. Occasionally a better place may be found
ready to hand, such as the bay-window illustrated
facing page 8 or such as that described in the
preceding chapter, or those mentioned in the first
chapter of Part II (page 146). The effort demanded will always be repaid many times by greater

ease and greater success in the management of
plants, and by the wider scope permitted.

TEMPERATURE

Next in importance to light, is the matter of
temperature. The ordinary house plants, to be
kept in health, require a temperature of sixty-five
to seventy-five degrees during the day and fifty to
fifty-five degrees at night. Frequently it will not
be possible to keep the room from going lower at
night, but it should be kept as near that as possible;
forty-five degrees occasionally will not do injury,
and even several degrees lower will not prove fatal,
but if frequently reached the plants will be checked
and seem to stand still. Plants in the dormant,
or semi-dormant condition are not so easily injured
by low temperature as those in full growth; also
plants which are quite dry will stand much more
cold than those in moist soil.

The proper condition of temperature is the most
difficult thing to regulate and maintain in growing
plants in the house. There is, however, at least
one room in almost every house where the night
temperature does not often go below forty-five or
fifty degrees, and if necessary all plants may be
collected into one room during very cold weather.
Another precaution which will often save them is
to move them away from the windows; put sheets
of newspaper inside the panes, not, however, touch-

ing the glass, as a " dead air space " must be left
between.   Where there is danger of freezing, a
kerosene lamp or stove left burning in the room
overnight will save them.   Never, when the temperature outside is below freezing, should plants be left
where leaves or blossoms may touch the glass.

As with the problem of light, so with that of
temperature — the specially designed place for
plants, no matter how small or simple a little nook
it may be, offers greater facility for furnishing the
proper conditions.   But it is, of course, not imperative, and as I have said, there is probably not one
home in twenty where a number of sorts of plants
cannot be safely carried through the winter.

MOISTURE

It would seem, at first thought, that the proper
condition of moisture could be furnished as easily
in the house as anywhere.   And so it can be as far
as applying water to the soil is concerned; but the
air in most dwellings in winter is terribly deficient
in moisture.   The fact that a room is so dry that
plants cannot live in it should sound a warning
to us who practically live there for days at a time,
but it does not, and we continue to contract all sorts
of nose and throat troubles, to say nothing of more
serious diseases.   No room too dry for plants to
live in is fit for people to live in.   Hot-air and steam
heating systems especially, produce an over-dry con-

dition of the atmosphere.   This can be overcome to a great or complete extent by thorough ventilation and by keeping water constantly where it can evaporate; over radiators, etc. This should be done for the sake of your own health, if not for that of the plant.

Further information as to watering and ventilation will be found in Chapter VII (page 45), but before we get anxious about just how to take care of plants we must know how to get them, and before getting them we must know what to give them to grow in — the plant's foundation.   So for a little we must be content with those prosaic but altogether essential matters of soil, manures and fertilizers, which in the next chapter I shall try to make clear in as brief manner as possible.

CHAPTER III

THE soil must furnish the whole foundation of plant life. For centuries those who have grown things have realized the vital importance of having the soil rich or well supplied with plant food; and if this is important in growing plants in the field or flower garden, where each vegetable or flower has from one to several cubic feet of earth in which to grow, how imperative it is to have rich soil in a pot or plant box where each plant may have but a few cubic inches!

But the trouble is not so much in knowing that plants should be given rich soil, as to know how to furnish it. I well remember my first attempt at making soil rich and thinking how I would surprise my grandmother, who worked about her plants in pots every day of her life, and still did not have them as big as they grew in the flower garden. I had seen the hired man put fertilizer on the garden. That was the secret! So I got a wooden box about two-thirds full of mellow garden earth, and filled most of the remaining space with fertilizer, well mixed into the soil, as I had seen him fix it. I remember that my anxiety was not that I get too much fertilizer in the soil, but that I would take so much out of the bag that it would be missed. Great indeed was my chagrin and disappointment, twelve hours after carefully setting out and watering my would-be prize plants, to notice that they had perceptibly turned yellow and wilted. And I certainly had made the soil rich.

So the problem is by no means as simple as might at first be supposed. Not only must sufficient plant food be added to the soil but it must be in certain forms, and neither too much nor too little may be given if the best results are to be attained.

Now it is a fact established beyond all dispute that not only food, but air and water, as well, must be supplied to the roots of growing plants; and this being the case, the *mechanical* condition of the soil in which the plant is to grow has a great deal to do with its success or failure. It must be what is termed a porous and friable soil — that is, one so light and open that water will drain through it without making it a compact, muddy mass. One of the things I noticed about my special fertilizer soil, mentioned above, was that it settled, after being watered, into a solid mass from which water would not drain and into which air could not penetrate.

It is next to impossible to find a soil just right for house plants, so, as a general thing the only way to get a good soil is to mix it yourself. For this purpose several ingredients are used. If you live

in a village or suburb, where the following may be
procured, your problem is not a difficult one.   Take
about equal parts of rotted sod, rotted horse manure
and leaf-mould from the woods and mix thoroughly
and together, adding from one-sixth to one-third,
in bulk, of coarse sand.   If a considerable quantity
of soil will be required during the year, it will be
well to have some place, such as a bin or large barrel, in which to keep a supply of each ingredient.
The sod should be cut three or four inches thick,
and stacked in layers with the grassy sides together,
giving an occasional soaking, if the weather is dry,
to hasten rotting.   The manure should be decomposed under cover, and turned frequently at first
to prevent burning out; or sod and manure can be
rotted together, stacking them in alternate layers
and forking over two or three times after rotting
has begun.   The manure furnishes plant food to
the compost, the rotted sod " body," the leaf-mould
water-absorbing qualities, and the sand, drainage
qualities.

If the soil is wanted at once, and no rotted sod is
to be had, use good garden loam, preferably from
some spot which was under clover-sod the year before.   If it is difficult to obtain well-rotted manure,
street sweepings may be used as a substitute, and
old chip-dirt from under the wood pile, or the bottom of the woodshed if it has a dirt floor, will do in
place of leaf-mould.   Peat, or thoroughly dried

and sweetened muck are also good substitutes for leaf-mould. Finely screened coal ashes may take the place of sand.

If you live in the city, where it is difficult to obtain and to handle the several materials mentioned, the best way is to get your soil ready mixed at the florists, as a bushel will fill numerous pots. If you prefer to mix it yourself, or to add any of the ingredients to the soil you may have, most florists can supply you with light soil, sand, peat or leaf-mould and rotted manure; and sphagnum moss, pots, saucers and other things required for your outfit. If a large supply is wanted, it would probably be cheaper to go to some establishment on the outskirts of the city where things are actually grown, than to depend upon the retail florist nearer at hand.

Potting soil when ready to use should be moist enough to be pressed into a ball by the hand, but never so moist as not to crumble to pieces again readily beneath the finger.

MANURES

Manure of some sort is essential to the growing of plants in pots or boxes, both because of the plant-food it adds to the soil, and because it improves its mechanical condition and sponginess or water-holding quality. Thoroughly rotted horse manure or horse and cow manure mixed is by far the best. Cow manure alone, or pig manure, is lumpy and

cold, and hen, sheep, pigeon or other special manures are not safe in the hands of the beginner, as
they are one-sided, being especially rich in nitrogen
and likely either to burn the plants or to cause too
soft and watery growth.

This brings us to the point where it is necessary
to say a few words about the theory of manures,
for they are not all alike and what would be wise
to give a plant under some circumstances under
others would be quite wrong, just as you would not
think of feeding beefsteak to a baby just recovering
from the colic, while it might be a very good thing
for a hungry man who was going to saw up your
wood-pile.

Plants of all sorts — in pots, in the garden or in
a ten-acre lot — require three kinds of food elements: nitrogen, phosphoric acid and potash.
These elements may be fed to the plants in various
forms; for instance, the nitrogen in hen manure, or
in cottonseed meal, or in salts from the nitrate fields
of Chile, known as nitrate of soda; the phosphoric
acid from bone, or from acid phosphate (a ground
rock treated with acid); the potash from wood ashes
or from German potash salts (muriate or sulphate
of potash).   Plants, to do their best, require that
all three elements shall be present in sufficient
amounts to supply their wants.

It is not necessary, however, to go very deeply
into the science of plant foods in order to grow

plants successfully. Fortunately, manure rotted as described above, furnishes all three elements in about the right proportions. Cow, sheep, hen and pigeon manure are best used as described later, under " Liquid Manuring."

FERTILIZERS

There are many brands of mixed fertilizers prepared specially for use in the greenhouse or on plants in pots. There is a temptation to use these on account of their convenient compact form, and because they are more agreeable to handle. As a general rule, however, much better results will be obtained by relying on rotted manure.

If you want to use fertilizers at all — and for certain purposes they will be very valuable — I would advise restricting the list to the following pure materials which are not mixed, and which are always uniform; nitrate of soda, cottonseed meal, pure fine ground bone, and wood ashes. (Several of the other chemicals are good, but not so commonly used.)

Ground bone is the most valuable of these. It should be what is known as " fine ground," or bone dust. It induces a strong but firm growth, and can be used safely in the potting soil, supplementing the manure as a source of plant food. From two to three quarts to a bushel of soil is the right amount to use. It should be thoroughly mixed through the

soil.   It may also be frequently used to advantage
as a top dressing on plants that have exhausted the
food in their pots, or while developing buds or
blooming.   Work two or three spoonfuls into the
top of the soil.

Nitrate of soda is the next in importance.   It is
very strong and must be carefully used, the safest
way being to use it as a liquid manure, one or two
teaspoonsful dissolved in three gallons of water.
If first dissolved in a pint of hot water, and then
added to the other, it will be more quickly done.
Use a pint or so of this solution in watering.   The
results will often be wonderful.

Cottonseed meal may be safely mixed with the
soil, like ground bone, but requires some time in
which to rot, before the plant can make use of it.

Wood ashes are also safe, and good to add to the
potting soil.   They help to make a firm, hard
growth, as a result of the potash they furnish.
Where plants seem to be making a too rapid,
watery growth, wood ashes may be applied to the
surface and worked in.

With a soil prepared as directed in the first part
of this chapter, there will be very little need for
using any other of the fertilizers, until plants have
been shifted into their last pots and have filled
them with roots.   When this stage is reached the
use of liquid manures as described later will frequently be beneficial.   If, however, a plant for any

reason seems backward, or slower in growth than it should be, an application or two of nitrate of soda will often produce results almost marvelous. Be sure, however, that your troubles are not due to some mistake in temperature, ventilation or watering, before you ascribe them to improper or exhausted soil.

Now, having had the patience to find out something about the conditions under which plants ought to succeed, let us proceed to the more interesting work of actually making them grow.

CHAPTER IV

ONE of the ways of getting a supply of plants for the house is to start them from seed. With a number of varieties, better specimens may be obtained by this method than by any other. Most of the annuals, and many of the biennials and perennials, are best reproduced in this way.

Simple as the art of starting plants from seed may seem, there are a number of things which must be thought of, and done correctly. We must give them a proper situation, soil, temperature, covering and amount of moisture, and when once above ground they need careful attention until lifted and started on their way as individual plants.

The number of plants of one sort which will be required for the house is naturally not large, and for that reason beginners often try starting their seeds in pots. But a pot is not a good thing to try to start plants in: the amount of earth is too small and dries out quickly. Seed pans are better, but even they must be watched very carefully. A wooden box, or flat, is better still. Cigar boxes are often used with good results; but a more satis-

factory way is to make a few regular flats from a
soap or cracker box bought at the grocer's.   Saw it
lengthwise into sections two inches deep, being careful to first draw out nails and wire staples in the
way, and bottom these with material of the same
sort.   Either leave the bottom boards half an inch
apart, or bore seven or eight half-inch holes in the
bottom of each, to provide thorough drainage.   If
they are to be used in the house, a coat or two of
paint will make them very presentable.   Of course
one such box will accommodate a great many seeds
— enough to start two hundred to a thousand little
plants — but you can sow them in rows, as described
later, and thus put from three to a dozen sorts in
each box.

Where most beginners fail in attempting to start
seeds is in not taking the trouble to prepare a proper
soil.   They are willing to take any amount of
trouble with watering and heat and all that, but
they will not fix a suitable soil.   The soil for the
seed box need not be rich, in fact it is better not to
have manure in it; but very porous and very light
it must be, especially for such small seeds as most
flowers have.   Such a soil may be mixed up from
rotted sod (or garden loam), leaf-mould and sharp
sand, used in equal proportions.   If the loam used
is clayey, it may take even a larger proportion of
sand.   The resulting mixture should be extremely
fine and crumbling, and feel almost " light as a

feather " in the hand.   If the sod and mould have
not already been screened, rub the compost through
a sieve of not more than quarter-inch mesh — such
as a coal-ash sifter.   This screening will help also
to incorporate the several ingredients evenly and
thoroughly.

While we provided holes in the seed box for
drainage, it is best to take even further precautions
in this matter by covering the bottom of the box
with nearly an inch of coarse material, such as the
roots and half decayed leaves, screened out of the
sods and leaf-mould.   On the top of this put the prepared soil, filling the box to within about a quarter
of an inch of the top, and packing down well into
the corners and along sides and ends.   The box
should not be filled level full, because in subsequent
waterings there would be no space to hold the water
which would run off over the sides instead of soaking down into the soil.

The usual way is to fill the boxes and sow the
seed, and then water the box on the surface, but I
mention here a method which I have used in my
own work for two years.   When filling the box, set
it in some place where it may be watered freely,
such as on the cellar floor, if too cold to work outdoors.   After putting in the first layer of coarse
material, give it a thorough soaking and then put
in about two-thirds of the rest of the soil required
and give that a thorough watering also.   The bal-

ance of the soil is then put in and made level, the
seeds sown, and no further watering given, or just
enough to moisten the surface and hold it in place,
if dry.   The same result can be obtained by filling
and sowing the box in the usual way, and then placing it in some place — such as the kitchen sink — in
about an inch of water, and leaving it until moisture, not water, shows upon the surface.   Either
of these ways is much surer than the old method
of trying to soak the soil through from the surface
after planting, in which case it is next to impossible
to wet the soil clear through without washing out
some of the small seeds.

After filling the box as directed, make the soil
perfectly smooth and level with a small flat piece of
board, or a brick.   Do not pack it down hard,—
just make it firm.   Then mark off straight narrow
lines, one to two inches apart, according to the size
of the seed to be sown.

The instructions usually given are to cover flower
seeds to from three to five times their own depth.
You may, if you like, take a foot-rule and try to
measure the diameter of a begonia or mignonette
seed; but you will probably save time by simply
trying to cover small seeds just as lightly as possible.   I mark off my seed rows with the point of a
lead pencil — which I have handy back of my ear
for writing the tags — sow the seed thinly, and as
evenly as possible by shaking it gently out of a

corner of the seed envelope, which is tapped lightly
with the lead pencil, and then press each row down
with the edge of a board about as thick as a shingle.
Over the whole scatter cocoanut fiber (which may
be bought of most seedmen) or light prepared soil,
as thinly as possible — just cover the seeds from
sight — and press the surface flat with a small piece
of board. A very light moistening, with a plant
sprinkler, completes the operation.

The temperature required in which to start the
seeds of any plant will be about the same as that
which the same plant requires when grown. Germination will be stronger and quicker, however, if
ten to fifteen degrees more, especially at night, can
be supplied. If this can be given as what the florists term " bottom heat," that is, applied under the
seed box, so much the better.

Until germination actually takes place, there is
little danger of getting the soil too warm, as it heats
through from the bottom very slowly. The box
may be placed on the steam radiator, on a stand
over the floor radiator, or on a couple of bricks on
the back of the kitchen range; or the box may be
supported over a lamp or small kerosene stove, care
being taken to have a piece of metal between the
wood and the direct heat of the flame. For the
first few days it may be kept in the shade, but as
soon as the seeds push through they must be given
all the light possible.

If the seed flats or pans are prepared by the newer method suggested above, they will probably not need any further watering, or not more than one, until the seeds are up. The necessity of further watering, in any case, will be shown by the soil's drying out on the surface. In the case of small seeds, such as most flower seeds are, the moisture in the soil will be retained much longer by keeping the box covered with a pane of glass, slightly raised at one side. If the box is to be kept in bright sunlight, shade the glass with a piece of paper, until the seedlings are up, which will be in a day or so with some sorts, and weeks with others.

From the time the little plants come up, until they are ready to prick off in other flats or into pots, the boxes should never be allowed to dry out. If they are being grown in winter or early spring, while the days are still short and the sun low, they will require very little water, and it should be applied only on bright mornings. In autumn and late spring, especially the latter, they will require more, and if the boxes dry out quickly, you should apply it toward evening. In either case, do not water until the soil is beginning to dry on the surface, and then water thoroughly, or until the soil will not readily absorb more. If you will take the pains, and have the facilities for doing it, by far the best way to keep the seed boxes supplied with moisture is to place them, when dry, in an inch or so of water (as described for seed sowing) and let them soak up what they need, or until the surface of the soil becomes moist.   This does the job more evenly and thoroughly than it can be done from the surface, and is also a safeguard against damping off, that dreaded disease of seedlings which is likely to carry away your whole sowing in one day — a decaying of the stem just at or below the soil.

From the time the seedlings come up they should be given abundance of light, and all the air possible while maintaining the required temperature.   It will be possible, except on very cold dark days, to give them fresh air.   Never, however, let a draft of air more than a few degrees colder than the room in which they are blow directly upon them.

The secret of growing the little plants until they are ready for their first shift is not so much in the amount of care given, as in its *regularity*.   Tend them every day — it will take only a few minutes time.   When the second true leaf appears they will be ready for their first change, which is described in Chapter VI.

A new scheme of sub-irrigation for flats. Some porous material such as sphagnum moss or excelsior (as here) is put on the open bottom and the flat watered by allowing it to stand in a sink or tub for a few minutes

Cuttings ready for the sand: the leaves have been clipped back.
From left to right, heliotrope, geranium, "patience plant"

Geranium cuttings ready to pot. Notice the roots, which
should not be allowed to grow more than half or three-
quarters of an inch long before potting

CHAPTER V

WHILE many plants are best started from seed, as described in the preceding chapter, there are many which cannot be so reproduced; especially named varieties which will not come true from seeds, but revert to older and inferior types.

Also it very frequently happens that one has a choice plant of some sort of which the seed is not to be obtained, and in this case also it becomes necessary to reproduce the plant in some other way.

Where large numbers of plants are to be started, and they may be had from seed, that is usually the best way in which to work up a supply: but where only a few are wanted, as for house plants or use in a small garden, propagation by cuttings is the quickest and most satisfactory method. Practically all of the house plants, including most of those which can be started from seed, may be increased in this way.

The matter of first importance, when starting plants by this system, is to have strong, healthy cuttings of the right degree of hardiness. Take your cuttings only from plants that are in full vigor, and growing strongly. They should be taken from what is termed " new growth," that is the terminal portions of shoots, which have not yet become old and hard. The proper condition of the wood may be determined by the following test: if the stem is bent between the fingers it should snap (like a green bean) ; if it bends and doubles without breaking it is either too old and will not readily root, or too soft and will be almost sure to wilt or rot.

The cutting should be from two to four inches long, according to the plant and variety to be propagated. It should be cut off slant-wise, as this will assist in its being pushed firmly down into the cutting box. It may be cut either near, or between a joint or eye — with the exception of a few plants, noted later. The lower leaves should be taken off clean; those remaining, if large, shortened back, as shown in the illustration facing page 29. Then the plant will not be so likely to wilt.

If the cuttings cannot be put in the propagating medium immediately after being made, keep them in the shade, and if necessary sprinkle to prevent wilting. I once obtained a batch of chrysanthemum cuttings from a brother florist who said that they were so badly wilted that they could never be rooted. I immersed them all in water for several hours, which revived them, and had the satisfaction of rooting almost every one.

The medium most commonly used in which to root cuttings is clean, medium-coarse sand, such as builders use. It must not be so fine as to pack tightly, nor so coarse as to fit loosely about the cuttings, and admit air so freely as to dry them out.

Make a flat similar to that used for starting seeds, but four or five inches deep. Place in the bottom an inch or two of gravel or coal ashes, covered lightly with moss or a single thickness of old bag, and then fill nearly full of clean sand. Make this level, and give a thorough soaking. After drying out for an hour or so, it is ready for the cuttings.

Mark the box off in straight lines, two or three inches apart, and insert the cuttings as closely as possible without touching, and to a depth of about one-third or one-half their length. A small, pointed stick, or dibber, will be convenient in getting them in firmly. Wet them down to pack the sand closely around them.

The best temperature for the room in which the cutting box is to be kept will be from fifty to fifty-five degrees at night. Like the seed box, however, it will be greatly helped by ten or fifteen degrees of bottom heat in addition. For method of giving this extra bottom heat, see page 26.

If the box is kept in a bright sunny place, shade the cuttings with a piece of newspaper during the heat of the day, to prevent wilting, and if the weather is so hot that the room is warmer than seventy degrees, an occasional light sprinkling will help to keep them fresh.

Never let the sand dry out or all your work will be lost. As a rule, it will require a thorough soaking every morning.

With these precautions taken, the cuttings should begin to throw out roots in from eight to twenty days, according to conditions and varieties. Do not let them stay in the sand after the roots form; it is much better to pot them off at once, before the roots get more than half an inch long. If some of the cuttings have not rooted but show a granulated condition where they were cut, they will be safe to pot off, as they will, as a rule, root in the soil.

The above method is the one usually employed. There is another, however, just as easy and more certain in results, especially where bottom heat cannot easily be had. It is called the " saucer " system of propagation. Make the cuttings as described above. Put the sand in a deep, water-tight dish, such as a glazed earthenware dish or a deep soup plate, and pack the cuttings in as thickly as necessary. Wet the sand to the consistency of mud and keep the dish in a warm light place. The temperature may be higher than when using the sand box, and there will not be a necessity for shading. *The sand must be kept constantly saturated:* that is the whole secret of success with this

method of rooting cuttings.   Pot them off as soon
as the roots begin to grow.

Cuttings made by the two systems described
above are usually taken in autumn, or in spring.
When it is necessary to get new plants during June,
July or August, a method called " layering in the
air " will have to be resorted to if you would be
certain of results.   Instead of taking the cutting
clean off, cut it nearly through; the smallest shred
of wood and bark will keep it from wilting, but it
should be kept upright, for if it hangs down the end
of the shoot will immediately begin to turn up,
making a U-shaped cutting.   The cuttings are left
thus partly attached for about eight days or until
they are thoroughly calloused, when they are taken
off and potted, like rooted cuttings, but giving a little more sand in the soil and not quite so much
water.   They are, of course, shaded for several
days.

Some of the plants ordinarily grown in the house,
such as Rex begonias, rubber plants, sword ferns,
are best increased by leaf cuttings, topping, layering
or other methods differing from seed sowing or
rooting cuttings.   These several operations will be
described in treating of the plants for which they
are used.

Having carried our little plants safely through
the first stage of their growth, it is necessary that
we use some care in getting them established as in-

dividuals, and give them the best possible preparation for successful service in their not unimportant
world.

CHAPTER VI

DIRECTIONS have already been given for preparing the best soil for house plants. This soil, sifted through a coarse screen — say a one-half inch mesh — is just right for " pricking off " or transplanting the little seedlings.

Use flats similar to those prepared for the seeds, but an inch deeper. In the bottom put an inch of the rough material screened from sods and manure. Give this a thorough watering; cover with an inch of the sifted soil, and wet this down also. Then fill the box nearly level full of the sifted soil, which should be neither dry nor moist enough to be sticky. Take care also that this soil is not much — if any — colder than the temperature in which the seedlings have been kept.

It is usually best to transplant the seedlings just as soon as they are large enough to be handled, which is as soon as the second true leaf appears. Nothing is gained by leaving them in the seed boxes longer, as they soon begin to crowd and get lanky and are more likely to be attacked by the damping off fungus than they are after being transferred.

35

Find a table or bench of the right height upon which to work comfortably. With a flat stick, or with a transplanting fork (which can be had for fifteen cents) lift a bunch of the little plants out, dirt and all, clear to the bottom of the box. Hold this clump in one hand and with the other gently tear away the seedlings, one at a time, discarding all crooked or weak ones. Never attempt to pull the seedlings from the soil in the flat, as the little rootlets are very easily broken off. They should come away almost intact, as shown facing page 48. Water the seed flats the day previous to transplanting, so that the soil will be in just the right condition, neither wet enough to make the roots sticky, nor so dry as to crumble away.

Take the little seedling by the stem between the thumb and forefinger, and with a small round pointed stick or dibber, or with the forefinger of the other hand, make a hole deep enough to receive the roots and about half the length — more if the seedlings are lanky — of the stem. As the little plant is dropped into place, the tips of both thumbs and forefingers, by one quick, firm movement, compress the earth firmly both down on the roots and against the stem so that the plant sticks upright and may not readily be pulled out. Of course there is a knack about it which cannot be put into words — I could have pricked off a hundred seedlings in the time I am spending in trying to describe the operation — but a little practice will make one reasonably efficient at it.

When the flat is completed, jar it slightly to level the surface and give a watering, being careful, however, to bend down the plants as little as possible. Set the plants on a level surface, and if the sun is bright, shade with newspapers during the middle of the day for two or three days.

From now on until ready for potting, keep at the required temperature, as near as possible, and water thoroughly on bright mornings when necessary, but only when the drying of the surface shows that the soil needs it. Above all, give all the air possible, while maintaining the necessary heat. The quality of the mature plants will depend more upon this precaution than upon anything else in the way of care.

The little seedlings are sometimes put from the seed flat directly into small pots. I strongly advise the method described above. The flats save room and care, and the plants do much better for a few weeks than they will in pots. Where room is scarce, it is well to transplant cuttings into flats instead of potting them off. As soon, however, as either the transplanted plants or cuttings begin to crowd in the flats, they must be put into pots. How soon this will be depends largely, of course, upon the amount of room they have been given. As many as a hundred are often set in a flat 13x19

inches, but it is well to give them twice as much
space as that if room permits.

POTTING

Cuttings and small plants are put into two-inch
or " thumb " pots.   Some of the larger growing
geraniums or very sturdy plants require two-and-
one-half inch pots, but the smaller size should be
used when possible.

The soil for pots up to three inches should be
screened, but not made too fine.   A coal-ash sifter,
or half-inch screen will do.   The soil should be
made up as directed in Chapter III.

The pots should be thoroughly cleaned with sand
and water, or by a several days' soaking, and then
wiping out with a cloth, if they have been used before.   An old pot, with dirt sticking to the inside
and the pores all clogged up, will not do good work.
Old or new, they should be immersed in water until
through bubbling just before using; otherwise they
will absorb too much moisture from the soil.

The method of potting should depend somewhat
upon the condition of the roots of the cutting.   If
they are less than half an inch long, as they should
be, fill the pot level full of soil, make a hole with
the forefinger of one hand; insert the cutting to
about half its depth with the other, rap the bottom
of the pot smartly against the bench to settle the
earth, and then press it down firmly with the thumbs,

leveling it as the pot is placed to one side in an empty flat. (The jarring down of the soil should precede the firming with the thumbs, as this will compact the soil more evenly within the pot.) This should leave the soil a little below the rim of the pot, making a space to hold water when watering; and the cutting should be so firmly embedded that it cannot be moved without breaking the soil.

With cuttings whose roots have been allowed to grow an inch or more in length, and plants with a considerable ball of roots — as they should have when coming from the transplanting flats — it is better partly to fill the pot. Hold the plant or cutting in position with the left hand and press the soil in about it with the right hand — firming it as directed in the former case. With a little practice either operation can be performed very rapidly. Florists do four to five hundred pots an hour.

When for any reason it is necessary to put a small or weakly rooted plant or cutting, or a cutting that is just on the point of sending forth roots, in a pot that seems too large, *put it near the edge of the pot,* instead of in the middle. This will often save a plant which would otherwise be lost, and at the next shift it can, of course, be put in the center of the pot.

If no small pots are at hand, several small plants or cuttings can be put around the edge of a four- or five-inch pot, with good results. Care must be taken, however, not to give too much water.

As soon as the little plants or cuttings are potted up, give them a thorough watering and place them where the holes in the bottoms of the pots will not be clogged with soil.   A large flat, in the bottom of which an inch of pebbles, coarse sand or sifted cinders has been put, will be a good place for them. Keep shaded during the hot part of the day for three or four days.   At first the pots may be placed as close together as possible, but in a very short time — two weeks at the most, if the growing conditions are right — they will need to be put farther apart. Nothing will injure them so quickly as being left crowded together where they cannot get enough air. Better, if necessary, give or throw away half of them than to attempt to grow fifty plants where you have room for only two dozen.

As before, water only when necessary, *i.e.,* when the surface of the soil begins to look whitish and dry. Then water thoroughly.   Until by practice you know just what they need, knock a few out of the pots, say fifteen minutes after watering, and see if the ball of earth has been wet through to the bottom; if not, you are not doing the job thoroughly.   If the pots do not dry out between waterings, but stay muddy and heavy, either your soil is not right or you have used pots too large for your plants.

REPOTTING

In the course of a week or two, if a plant is

Potted cuttings ready for shifting to a larger pot. From left
to right, ivy geranium, snapdragon, geranium and dusty miller

Some plants, like Rex begonia, will strike root from their
leaves if perforated with a knife into damp sand

In all potted plants an important detail is the placing of rough
drainage material, such as broken pieces of pot, charcoal,
ashes, etc., at the bottom, to prevent moisture from settling
in the soil and souring it

knocked out, the small white roots may be seen coming through the ball of earth and beginning to curl around the outside of it. The time for repotting the young plants will have been reached when these roots have made a thick network around the ball of earth, but before they become brown and woody; that is, while they are still white and succulent — " working roots," as the florists term them.

The shift, as a general rule, should be to a pot only one size larger, that is, from a three to a four, or a four to a five.

Remove the plant from the old pot by holding the stem of the plant between the index and middle finger of the left hand, and with the right inverting the pot and rapping the edge of the rim sharply against the edge of the bench or table.

Before putting the plant into the new pot, remove the top half inch of soil and gently loosen up the lower half of the ball of roots, if it is firmly matted.

Put soil in the bottom of the pot to such a depth that when the ball of roots is covered with half an inch or so of new soil, the surface thereof will still be about half an inch below the rim of the pot. Hold the plant in place with the left hand, and with the right fill in around it, making the soil firm as before. Water and care is the same as after the first potting.

Pots four inches or over in size should be crocked to make certain of sufficient drainage. The best

material to use is broken charcoal, in pieces one-half
to an inch in diameter.   Pieces of broken pots, cinders or rough pebbles will do.   Be sure that the
drainage hole is not covered; if pieces of pots are
used, put the concave side down over the hole, as illustrated facing page 41.   The depth of the drainage
material, or crocking, will be from half an inch to
three inches, according to the size of the pot.   Over
this rough material put a little screenings, leaf
mould or sphagnum moss, to prevent the soil's washing down into it.   Then fill in with soil and pot in
the regular way.

The time for repotting house plants is at the beginning of their growing season.   It varies, of
course, with the different kinds.   The great majority, however, start into new growth in the spring
and should be repotted from the middle of March
to the middle of May.   Plants kept through the
winter for stock plants are usually started up and repotted early in February to induce the abundant new
growth that furnishes cuttings.   The method
of repotting will depend on the nature of the plant.
Soft-wooded plants, like geraniums, are put in in the
ordinary way and firmed with the fingers.   The
palms do best with the new soil more firmly packed
about the old ball of roots.   Hard-wooded plants
with very fine roots, like the azaleas, should have
the soil rammed down firmly about the old ball; for
which purpose it is necessary to use a blunt, flat

piece of wood, of convenient size. In repotting such plants, it is well to let the ball of roots soak several minutes in a pail of water before putting into the new pot. If very densely matted, make several holes in it with a spike, working it around, and leave the soil a little lower at the center of the pot to induce the water to run down through the root ball.

Plants that have been crocked in the old pots should have this material removed, if possible, before going into their new quarters.

Plants in large pots often use up all the plant food available, and where they cannot be given still larger pots become quite a problem. They are usually handsome specimens which one does not like to lose. Remove such a plant from its pot and carefully *wash* all the soil from the roots; clean the pot and carefully repot in fresh soil in the same pot. The result will be extremely satisfactory.

Until one has become proficient in the art of potting, it will pay well to practice with every plant and cutting that may be had. If you have mistakes to make, make them with these, so that your favorite plants may be handled safely.

CHAPTER VII

MANAGEMENT OF HOUSE PLANTS

THERE are some general rules that will apply to taking care of all plants in the house; then there are several groups, the different sorts in which are handled more or less alike; and lastly there are the individual requirements of the plants in the several groups to be considered.

Information about all these varieties, as given in the usual way, results in a more or less confusing mass of detail. It is for the purpose of getting this information into as plain a form as possible that the instructions in the first chapters of this book have been given in such detail; and those instructions should be used in conjunction with the following pages. The beginner cannot expect to fully comprehend the suggestions given until the plain everyday operations of plant growing have become familiar.

Much of what has been said in the previous pages has borne upon the several points of managing plants successfully in the house. It will be of use, however, to have those various suggestions brought together in condensed form.

In the first place it must be remembered that at best it is hard to get conditions in the living-room that will be suitable for the healthy growth of plants. Every effort should be made to prepare a place for them in which such conditions may be made as nearly ideal as possible: plenty of light, evenly regulated temperature; moisture in the air.

For most house plants the temperature should be 50 to 55 at night and 65 to 75 during the day. An occasional night temperature of 45 or even 40 will not do great harm but if reached frequently will check the growth of the plants.

Air should be given every day when the temperature of the room will not be too greatly lowered thereby. Avoid direct drafts, as sudden chills are apt to produce bad results. Even on very cold days, fresh air may be let in indirectly, through a window open in an adjoining room or through a hall. It is better, when possible, to give a little ventilation during an hour or two, than to rush too sudden a lowering of the temperature by trying to do it all in fifteen minutes.

The amount of water which should be given will depend both upon the plant and upon the season. During the dull days of winter and during the " resting season " of all plants, very little water will be required. It should be given on bright mornings. During early fall and late spring, when the pots or boxes dry out very rapidly, water in the evening. In either case, however, withhold water until the soil is beginning to get on the " dry side " and then water thoroughly. Water should be given until it runs down through into the saucers but should not be allowed to remain there.

Sometimes it will be beneficial to moisten the foliage of plants without wetting the soil. Just after repotting and in fighting plant lice, red spider and other insect enemies (see Chapter XVII) this treatment will be necessary. A fine-rose spray on the watering-can may be used but a rubber plant-sprinkler costing about sixty-five cents, will be very much better, as with it the water will be applied in a finer spray with a great deal more force and to either the upper or under surface of the leaves — a point of great importance.

Plants growing in windows, where the light strikes them only, or mostly, from one side, should be frequently turned to prevent their growing one-sided

Also do not hesitate to use knife, scissors and fingers in keeping them symmetrical and shapely. One of the greatest mistakes that amateurs make is in being afraid to cut an ungainly or half leafless branch. Instead of injuring a plant, such pruning frequently is an actual benefit.

If neglected, dust will quickly gather on the leaves and clog their pores, and as the plants have no way of breathing but through their leaves, you

can see what the result must be. Syringing, mentioned above, will help. They should also be wiped
clean with a soft dry cloth, especially such plants
as palms, rubbers, Rex begonias. Do *not* use olive
oil or any other sticky substance on the cloth. Always remove at once any broken, dead or diseased
leaf or flower. Do not let flowering plants go to
seed: nothing else will so quickly bring the blooming period to a close.

Do not try to force your plants into continuous
growth. Almost without exception they demand
a period of rest, and if you do not allow them to
take it when nature suggests, they will take it
themselves when you do not want them to. The
natural rest period is during the winter. During
this time a *very* little water will do and no repotting
or manuring should be attempted.

It is, however, desirable in some cases, as with
many of the flowering plants, to change the season
bloom, as we want their beauty during the winter.
In such cases they should be *made* to rest during
the summer, by withholding water and keeping
them disbudded.

Many beginners get the idea that as soon as any
plant has filled its pot with roots it must be immediately shifted to a larger one. While this is as
a rule true with small plants, being grown on, it is
not at all true of mature plants, especially those
wanted to bloom in the house. When a shift has

been given, at the beginning of the growing period, no further change should be necessary during the winter.   It will, however, be well, if not imperative, to furnish food in the form of liquid manures when the soil in the pot has become filled with roots.   It should be applied from one to three times a week — the former being sufficient for a plant showing ordinary growth.

All the animal manures, cow, horse, sheep, hen, etc.,— are good to use in this way, but cow manure is the safest and best.   Place three or four inches of half-rotted manure in a galvanized iron pail, fill with water, and after standing a few hours it will be ready for use.   The pail can be refilled. As long as the liquid becomes the color of weak tea it will be strong enough to use.   Give from a gill to a pint at each application to a six- or eight-inch pot.   The other manures should not be made quite so strong.   For liquid chemicals see page 19 or mix up the following: 5 lbs. nitrate of soda, 3 of nitrate of potash and 2 of phosphate of ammonia, and use 1 oz. of the mixture dissolved in five or six gallons of water.

At the beginning of the growing period and at frequent intervals during the early growth of plants they must be repotted.   The operation is described on page 40.

As soon as danger of late frost is over in the spring the plants should be got out of the house.   It

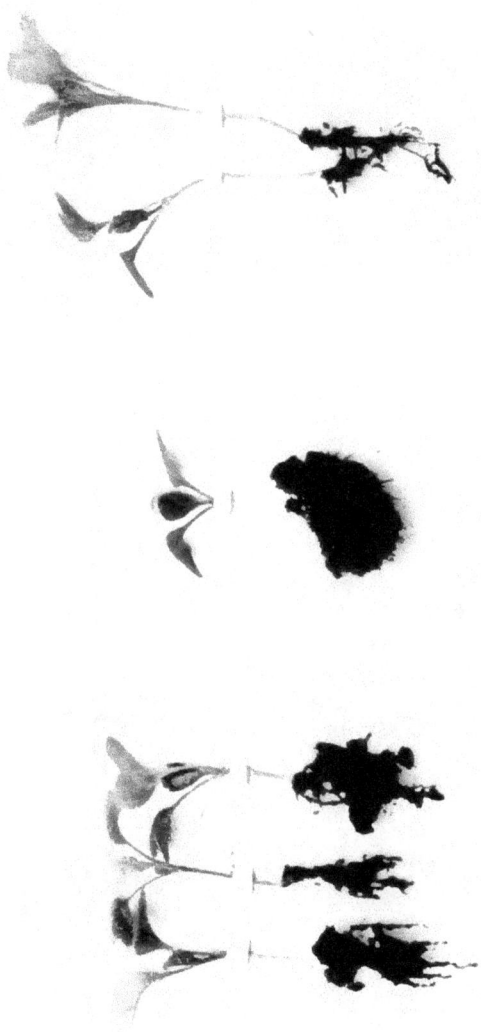

From left to right, cabbage seedlings just right for transplanting; seedlings of stocks; lanky seedlings that have been too thickly sown These last should be set deeply, as indicated by the cross line

An attractive and efficient flower bay was made here by water-
proofing the floor, building plant shelves and isolating the
whole when necessary with the curtains

is safest to " harden them off " first by leaving them
a few nights with the windows wide open or in a
sheltered place on the veranda.   Those which require partial shade may be kept on the veranda or
under a tree.   Most of them, however, will do best
in the full sun and should, if wanted for use in
the house a second season, be kept in their pots.
The best way to handle them is to dig out a bed six
or eight inches deep (the sod and earth taken out
may be used in your dirt heap for next year) and
fill it with sifted coal ashes.   In this, " plunge," that
is, bury the pots up to their rims.   If set on the surface of the soil it will be next to impossible to keep
them sufficiently wet unless they are protected from
the direct rays of the sun by an overhead screening
of lath nailed close together, or " protecting cloth "
waterproofed.   Where   many   plants   are   grown
for the house such a shed, open on all sides, is sometimes made.

Care must be taken not to let plants in " plunged "
pots root through into the soil.   This is prevented
by lifting and partly turning the pots every week
or so.   They will not root through into the coal
cinders as rapidly as into soil and better drainage
is secured.   Watch the soil in the pots, not that in
which they are plunged, when deciding about watering.   For most plants a thorough watering, tops
and all, once every afternoon ordinarily will not be
too much.

Plants such as geraniums and heliotrope, which are wanted for blooming in early winter, should be kept rather dry and all buds pinched off.   Do not shift them to new pots until two or three weeks before time to take them in.

CHAPTER VIII

FLOWERING PLANTS

THE very important question — " What plants shall be grown in the house? "— must be left for the individual to answer. In selecting a few to describe somewhat in detail in the first part of this chapter, I do not mean to imply that the others are not as beautiful, or may not, with proper care, be successfully grown in the house. However, most of those described are the more popular — very possibly because as a rule greater success is attained with them.

The same is true of the treatment of the other groups — shrubs, foliage plants, palms, ferns, vines, cacti and bulbs, which are classed not upon a strict botanical basis but with reference to their general habits and requirements, my sole object in this book being to make the proper cultural directions as definite and clear as possible.

Begonias

I think if I were restricted to the use of one class of plants for beautifying my home in winter I should without hesitation choose the begonias.

No other plants so combine decorative effect, beauty of form and flower, continuity of bloom and general ease of culture.

There are three types: the flowering fibrous-rooted begonias, the decorative leaved begonias and the tuberous-rooted, with their abundant and gorgeous flowers and beautiful foliage. (These latter are described more fully in Chapter XV on Bulbs.)

Begonias are rather difficult to raise from seed and the best way to get them is to go to some good florist and select a few specimens; after that you can easily keep supplied by cuttings (see page 29). The large fancy-leaved begonias (Rex begonias) are increased by "leaf-cuttings." Take an old leaf and cut it into triangular pieces, about three inches each way and with a part of one of the thick main ribs at one corner of each piece; this is the corner to put into the sand. These — seven or eight of which can be made from one leaf — should be inserted about an inch into the sand of the cutting box or saucer, and treated as ordinary cuttings. The new growth will come up from the rib. (Illustration facing page 40). Some of the foliage begonias have long, thick stems, or " rhizomes " growing just above the soil; from these the leaves grow. Propagate by cutting the rhizome into pieces about two inches long and covering in the rooting medium.

The most satisfactory way to select your be-

gonias is to see them actually growing at the florist's. In case selection cannot be made, thus, however, the following brief descriptions may be helpful. The begonia with the most showy flowers
is the "coral" begonia — (in catalogues *B. macu-
lata,* var. Corallina). The flowers, which grow in
large clusters, reach half an inch across.

Begonias *rubra,* Alba, Vernon, *nitida* and *N.
alba,* Luminosa, Sandersoni and *semperflorens, gi-
gantea rosea,* are all good sorts.

For foliage, *Begonia metallica,* is the most popular. The flowers while not conspicuous are very
pretty. *B. Thurstoni, albo-picta,* and *argenteo-
guttata* are also very attractive, the two latter having small silvery spots upon the leaves.

Of the large leaved Rex begonias new varieties
are frequently introduced. They are seldom improvements over the old favorites, Philadelphus,
Silver Queen, Fire King, Mrs. Rivers and others.

One of the most glorious of all flower sights is a
plant of begonia Gloire de Lorraine in full bloom.
It makes a graceful hanging mass of the most
beautiful pink flowers. I cannot, however, con-
scientiously recommend it as a house plant. The
best way is to get a plant, say in October, which is
just about to bloom. Even if you lose it after it
is through blooming — they continue in flower for
several months — it will have been well worth the
expense. But it is not necessary to lose it. When

through flowering give it less water and keep in a cool light place. During summer keep it as cool as possible, on the veranda, or plunged in the shade of a tree. About September rapid growth will be made and it may gradually be given full sunlight.

Gloire Cincinnati is a splendid begonia of very recent introduction and it is claimed to be much hardier than Gloire de Lorraine, but whether it will prove satisfactory as a house plant I cannot say.

There are many other beautiful kinds of begonias besides the few described above. If you have room, by all means try some of them.

As to soil, add about one-third of thoroughly pulverized leaf-mould to the potting soil described on page 15, if you would give them the best conditions. In watering keep them if anything a little on the " dry side." They like plenty of light but will do best if kept out of the direct rays of the sun.

Fuchsia.

There is perhaps no plant which more perfectly combines gracefulness and beauty of color than a well grown fuchsia in full bloom. Well-grown in this case does not simply mean that it should have been given the proper care as regards food and temperature. The fuchsia is naturally a somewhat trailing and very brittle-wooded plant. It needs support and the problem is to give it this support

and at the same time not destroy its natural gracefulness of form, as is usually done when it is tied
up stiffly to a wooden stake.   If tied carefully to an
inconspicuous green stake by means of green twine
this may be accomplished.   A better way will be
to use one of the stakes described on page 144.

Fuchsias are shade plants.   The full direct sunlight is likely to prove fatal to their existence.   In
winter they may be kept in an east or north window, or on the inside of other plants in a south window.   If they are wanted to bloom early in the fall
keep well pinched back and disbudded during the
summer which is the natural blooming season for
all the best varieties.   For summer blooming, dry
off gradually in the fall and keep during the winter — until February or March — in a frost-proof
room or cellar.   After they have been brought into
the light, repot and water and new growth will
start.   Prune back the old branches severely, as the
next crop of flowers will be borne on the new wood.
This is also a good time to start cuttings for a new
supply of plants.

Old plants — two or three years — will, however,
give a far greater abundance of flowers.

The most serious enemy of the fuchsia indoors is
the pernicious red spider.   For details of the proper
reception to be given him see page 134.

The varieties of the fuchsia, in both single and
double flowers, are many.   Among popular sorts

are Elm City, Black Prince, speciosa, Phenomenal.
Florists' catalogues list many others, new and for
the most part well worth trying.

Geraniums.

The geranium has been for years, and is likely
to remain, the most popular flowering plant of all,
whether for use in summer flower beds or for the
winter window garden.   To some people this wide
popularity renders it less desirable, but with those
who grow plants for their intrinsic beauty and not
because they may or may not be in vogue the geranium with its healthy vitality, its attractive foliage
and its simply marvelous range of color and delicate shadings will always be a favorite.   I even
venture to predict more; to prophesy that it is going
to be used, as one seldom sees it now, as a cut flower
for decorative purposes.   I have grown some of the
newer varieties with stems from twelve to eighteen
inches long, supporting enormous trusses of dull
red or the most delicate pink and keeping fresh in
vases for days at a time.   I find that very few people, even old flower lovers, have any conception of
the improvement and variety which the last few
years have brought, especially in the wonderful new
creations coming from the hands of the French hy-
bridizers.   The latest news is that a German plant-
breeder has produced the first of a new race of
Pelargoniums (Pansy or Lady Washington gera-

niums) that continues to bloom as long as any of our
ordinary bedding sorts.   It has not yet been offered
in this country, but doubtless soon will be, and it
will be an acquisition indeed.

The culture of the geranium is simple.   For its
use as a house plant there are just two things to
keep in mind; first give it a soil which is a little on
the heavy side; that is, use three parts of good heavy
loam, one of manure and one of sand; secondly do
not over-water.   Keep it on the " dry side " —
(see page 45).

To have geraniums blooming in the house *all*
winter prepare plants in two ways, as follows:
First, in May or June pot up a number of old
plants.   Cut back quite severely, leaving a skeleton
work of old wood, well branched, from which the
new flowering wood will grow.   Keep plunged and
turned during the summer and take off every bud
until three or four weeks before you are ready to
take the plants inside.   Secondly, in March or
April, start some new plants from cuttings and
grow these, with frequent shifts, until they fill six-
or seven-inch pots, but keep them pinched back to
induce a branching growth, and disbudded, until
about the end of December.   These will come into
bloom after the old plants.

The best time for propagating the general supply of geraniums is from September 15th to the end
of October.   Cuttings should be taken from wood

that is as firm and ripe as possible, while still yielding to the " snapping test " (see page 30). In all
stages of growth the geranium is remarkably free
from any insect or disease.

The varieties of geraniums now run into the
hundreds — a wonderful collection. I shall name
but a few, all of which I know from my own experience in selling several thousand every spring,
are sure to be well-liked and good bloomers.

Geranium Varieties

S. A. Nutt leads them all. It is the richest,
darkest crimson — usually ordered as " the darkest red." It is a great bloomer, but one word of
caution where you grow your own plants:—You
must keep it cut back and make it branch, otherwise
it will surely grow up tall and spindling. E. H.
Trego is the most brilliant of the reds that I
have grown. Marquis de Castellane is the richest
of the reds — a dull, even, glowing color with what
artists term " warmth " and " depth." The trusses
are immense and the stems long, stiff and erect. It
is the best geranium for massing in bouquets that I
know.

Beauté Potevine is the richest, most glorious of
the salmon pinks — perhaps the most popular of all
the geraniums as a pot plant for the house. It is a
sturdy grower and a wonderful bloomer.

Dorothy Perkins is a strong growing bright pink,

with an almost white center. Very attractive.

Roseleur is one of the most lovely delicate pinks. Mme. Récamier, perhaps the best of the double whites, making a very compact, sturdy plant.

Silver-leafed Nutt, very recently introduced, is, I believe, destined to be one of the most popular of all geraniums. It has the rich flowers of S. A. Nutt and leaves of a beautiful dull, light green, bordered with silver white. I am chary of novelties, and got my first plants last spring with the expectation of being disappointed. So far it has proved a great acquisition.

New-life is another new sort which has won great popularity, the center of the flowers being white in contrast to the red of the outer petals. This is one of a new type of geranium having two more or less distinct colors in each flower. Another new type is the " Cactus " section, with petals narrower and recurved. In fact, the geranium seems to have by no means reached its full development.

Foliage Geraniums. The foremost of these is Mme. Salleroi (Silver-leaf geranium). It is unequaled as a border and for mingling with other plants in the edge of boxes and vases. Well grown specimens make beautiful single pot plants. Mrs. Pollock and Mountain of Snow are other good varieties.

Sweet Scented Geranium. This type has two

valuable uses; their delicious fragrance and also the
beauty and long keeping quality of the leaves when
used in bouquets or to furnish green with geranium
blossoms.   Rose and Lemon (or Skeleton) are the
two old favorites of this type.   The Mint geranium,
with a broad, large leaf of a beautiful soft green,
and thick velvety texture, should be better known.
All three must be kept well cut back, as they like
to grow long and scraggly.

The ivy-leafed geraniums have not yet come into
their own.   To me they are the most beautiful of
all.   The leaves are like ivy leaves, only thicker
and more glossy.   The flowers, which are freely
borne, contain some of the most beautiful and delicate shades and markings of any flowers, and the
vines are exceedingly graceful in habit when given
a place where they can spread out or hang down.
Like the common or Zonal geranium, the ivy-leafed
section has within the last few years been greatly
improved.   There is space here to mention but one
variety (L'Elegantea), whose variegated white and
green foliage, in addition to its lovely flowers, gives
it a wonderful charm.

The Pelargoniums (Pansy Geraniums) — This
section contains the most wonderful flowers of all
the geraniums.   Imagine, if you can, a rather
graceful shrub with attractive foliage, eighteen
inches or so high and broad, covered with loose
clusters of pansies in the most brilliant and har-

Begonias combine more fully than any other house plant the three important factors of beauty of form and flower, continuity of bloom and ease of culture. This is the variety Pride of Cincinnati

Primula obconica. Primroses need no particular care. Buy small plants from the florist each spring

The pansy geraniums bear the most beautiful flowers of the whole geranium family, but as yet the flowering season is rather short

monious contrasts of color, and the most delicate
blendings of rare shades, such as snow white and
lilac.   Unfortunately, these marvelous blossoms remain but a few weeks at most, and then there is a
year's care and waiting.   As with the fantastic
cacti, all their blossoming energy and beauty seems
to be concentrated into one brief but glorious effort.
It certainly is to be hoped that the new strain, mentioned on a former page, will successfully be developed.   Pelargoniums are propagated by cuttings,
and cared for as the ordinary geraniums, except
that they should be kept very cold and dry during
their winter resting spell.   Cut back after blooming.

Heliotrope

The heliotrope has long been the queen of
all flowers grown for fragrance.   It is grown
readily from either seeds or cuttings; the latter generally rooted in the spring.   For blooming in winter, start young plants in February, or
cut back old ones after flowering, and keep growing
but pinched back and disbudded, in partial shade
during the summer.

There are several varieties, from dark purple to
very light and white.   Lemoine's hybrids have the
largest flowers, but are not so fragrant as some of
the smaller sorts.

By pinching off the side shoots and training to a
single main stalk, the plants may be grown as for-

mal standards, with the flowering branches several feet from the pot, like the head of a tree. For certain uses they are appropriate, but I think not nearly as beautiful as when well trimmed to shape and grown in the ordinary way.

The heliotrope objects to any sudden change, whether of temperature, watering or soil, and will readily turn brown and drop all its leaves. Giving it proper care and cutting back, however, will quickly bring it into good humor again.

Petunia

The petunia is one of the most easily grown and generous bloomers of all house plants. It is, however, a little coarse and some people object to its heavy odor. The flowers are both single and double, each having its advocates. Both have been vastly improved within the last few years. Certain it is that some of the new ruffled giant singles are remarkably beautiful, even as individual flowers; and the new fringed doubles, which come in agreeable shades of pink, variegated to pure white (instead of that harsh magenta which characterized the older style) produce beautiful mass effects with their quantities of bloom.

They are grown either from seed or cuttings, the latter frequently blooming in the cutting box, if allowed to. In raising seedlings, be sure to save all the slowest growing and delicate looking plants,

as they are fairly sure to give some of the best flowers, the worthless singles growing strong and rank
from the start. Plants growing outdoors during the
summer may be cut back, potted up and started into
new growth. The singles bloom more freely than
the doubles, especially indoors. After blooming,
cut the plants back to within a few inches of the
root, repot or give liquid manure and a new growth
will be sent up, and soon be in blossom again.

Primroses

Of the deservedly popular primrose there
are two types, the Chinese primrose *(Primula Sinensis)* and *Primula obconica.* Both
are favorites, because of their simple beauty and
the remarkable freedom and constancy with which
they bloom. Another advantage is that they do
not require direct sunlight. Primroses need no
particular care. The soil may have a little extra
leaf-mould and should slope toward the edges of
the pot, to prevent the possibility of any water
collecting at the crown of the plant, which must be
left well above the soil when potting.

The easiest way to get plants is to buy small
ones from the florist every spring. They may be
raised from seed successfully, however, if one will
take care to give them a shaded, cool location during
the hot summer months, such as a coldframe covered with protecting cloth, or any light material

that will freely admit air.   From seed sown in February or March they should be ready to bloom by the following Christmas.   It does not pay to keep the plants over for a second season.

There are numerous varieties.   One very small sort, *P. Forbesi* — sometimes caled Baby Primrose — is exceedingly floriferous.   Several plants of this sort put together in a large pan make a most beautiful sight, and will do well as a decoration for a center table.

Until recently *P. obconica* was inferior in size of flower to the Chinese primrose, but the newer strains, under the name *P. grandiflora fimbriata,* or Giant Fringed, are quite wonderful.   Some of the individual flowers are over an inch and a quarter across, and range from pure white to deep rose. If you cannot obtain other plants of this type from your florist they will well repay the trouble of starting from seed.

Snapdragon

I   feel   somewhat   doubtful   about   giving this comparatively little known flower a place among the especially recommended plants.   Not on the basis of my own experience with it, but because in the several books in my possession which deal with house plants, I do not find it mentioned. There certainly can be no question that the long spikes of flowers in pure white, light and dark reds,

deep wines and clear yellows, with combinations
of two or more of these in many cases, are among
our most beautiful flowers. They stay in blossom
a long time, each stalk opening out slowly from the
bottom to the top of the spike, like a gladiolus.
They seem, in my own experience at least, to stand
almost any amount of abuse; this spring several old
plants that I had abandoned to their fate insisted on
coming to life again and trying to vie with their
younger progeny in flowering.

Snapdragons are easily raised from seed, or propagated by cuttings. For winter blooming sow the
former in March or April, grow on in a cool place
and keep pinched back to make bushy plants. If
you have limited room, let one stalk blossom on
each plant, so that you can avoid selecting dupli-
cates. Cuttings may be taken at any time when the
weather is not too hot. Take the tops of flowering
shoots which have not yet matured so far as to become hollow.

The varieties have been greatly improved, that
now sold as Giant-flowered Hybrids being the best.
There is also a dwarf type and of still later introduction a double white. This will undoubtedly
break into the other colors and give us a valuable
new race.

With the directions given for the foregoing, and
also on pages 6 to 50, the following brief instructions should be necessary to enable success with the

other flowering plants which are worth trying in the house for winter blooming.

Ageratum—Valuable for its bright blue flowers and dwarf growth, going in well with other plants. There is also a white variety. Make cuttings in August, or cut back and pot up old plants.

Alyssum—Good with other plants to produce a light bouquet-like effect. White. Fall and dwarf varieties. Seed or cuttings.

Balsam—Beautiful colors. Take up and pot after blooming in garden. Only double sorts worth while.

Candytuft—Colors. Good for cut flowers. Seed or cuttings.

Cannas—New dwarf hybrids, named varieties have beautiful flowers. Give rich soil, lots of sun and water. Dry off after flowering.

Carnation—This beautiful flower is not well adapted for house culture. It may, however, be grown in five-or-six-inch pots, using a heavy soil, keeping in a cool temperature, about forty-five degrees at night, watering regularly and spraying daily with as much force as possible. For further information about growing the plants, see Part II., page 181.

Carnation Marguerite—These are much better suited for the trials of house culture. While not

as large, they are in other respects fully as beautiful. Take up the best sorts from the flower garden,
cut back severely and keep shaded until new growth
starts.

Chrysanthemum—This is another beautiful
flower not well suited to house culture. However,
if you have room,— it will take an eight-, nine- or
even ten-inch pot for each plant — and want to go
to the trouble, you can have it indoors. For cultural directions see Part II, page 185.

Daisies, Double English Daisies—The bright little short-stemmed daisies, seen so frequently in
spring (*Bellis perennis*) are not often used as a
house plant, but make a very agreeable surprise.
Start from seed in August; transplant to boxes of
suitable size, and on the approach of freezing
weather cover gradually with leaves and rough manure or litter in a sheltered, well drained place.
Bring them in as wanted from January on.

Daisy, Paris or Marguerite—Beautiful daisy-
like flowers, very freely borne, in two colors, pure
white and delicate yellow. Root cuttings in spring
and keep pinched back for winter flowering. Grow
in rather heavy rich soil, with plenty of water.

Patience Plant (Impatiens)—This old-fashioned
but cheery flowered plant resembles the flowering begonias in looks and habit. It grows very rapidly
and is one of the most indefatigable bloomers of all
plants. Spring cuttings grown on will make good

flowering plant for winter.   Give plenty of water.

Lobelia—This favorite little plant bears starry blossoms of one of the most intense blues found anywhere in the realm of flowers.   Grown easily from fall sown seed, or cuttings.   Star of Ishmael and Kathreen Mallard are two named varieties recently introduced and great improvements.

Mahernia—(Honey-bell)—Of great value for its fragrance.   Grow on from summer cuttings.

Mignonette—Another flower owing its popularity to its fragrance.   Start winter plants by sowing in two-inch pots in July or August, several seeds to a pot.   As soon as well started, thin to the best plant.   Grow on, keeping cool and well pinched back.   Give support.   There are several newer named varieties that are great improvements over the old type, especially in size of spike.   Colossal, Allan's Defiance, Machet, are all fine sorts.

Pansy—If wanted for winter blooming, take cuttings or start from seed, as described for Daisy *(Bellis perennis)*.   The seed bed must be kept cool and shaded.

Salvia—One of the most brilliant of all flowering plants.   For winter make cuttings in August, or take off suckers with roots at base of plant.   They like heat.   Keep thoroughly sprayed to ward off red spider.

Piqueria or Stevia serrata—Another fragrant flower.   Root cuttings in January or February and grow on for blooming from November to February.

Stocks—What I said abut snapdragons on page 64 might well be repeated here. Start from seed in August or September. They are very easily grown. In addition to their beauty — they resemble a spray of small roses — is their entrancing fragrance. Only the double sorts are good. There are many fine new sorts. Abundance, a beautiful delicate pink, will be sure to arouse your enthusiasm.

Verbena—If any of these old brilliant favorites are wanted, start from cuttings, being sure to use strong new growth which may be induced by spading up and enriching the soil in August, and cutting back the plants.

Verbena, Lemon — See page 77.

Violets—See Part II (page 183).

There is one thing which the beginner cannot be told too often, and which I repeat here, as it has much to do with the success of many of the above plants. Do not fail to pinch back seedlings and cuttings during their early stages of growth, to induce the formation of stocky, well-branched plants. This must be the foundation of the winter's returns.

CHAPTER IX

SHRUBS

THE shrubs of dwarf habit available for growing inside in winter are numerous and valuable. They include a number of the most attractive plants one may have, and as a rule will stand more hardships in the way of poor light, low temperature and irregular attention than any of the other flowering plants.

They differ from the other flowering plants in several ways. They are harder wooded; the resting spell is more marked and they make growth and store up energy for flowering *ahead* of the blossoming season.

Their differences in habit of growth naturally involve differences in treatment. In the first place, they are harder to propagate; in many cases it is better for the amateur to get plants from the florist than to try to raise them. This is not such a disadvantage as might at first appear, because most of them can be kept for several years, only improving with age.

The " snapping " test (page 30) will not apply to many of the shrubs when taking cuttings. In

this case they are made from the new growth after
it becomes firm and well ripened. It should be
fresh and plump, and rooting will be made more
certain by bottom heat. Often cuttings of hard-
wooded plants, such as oleander, are rooted in plain
water, in wide-mouthed bottles hung in a warm
place in the sun, the water being frequently renewed
or kept fresh with a lump or so of charcoal.

Many of the shrubs are beautiful for summer
blooming on the veranda or in large pots or tubs.
These may be kept over winter safely by drying off
and keeping in a frost-proof cellar where they will
get little light. In this way they will come out
again in the spring, just as hardy shrubs do out-of-
doors. The earth should not be allowed to get dust
dry, but should not be more than slightly moist;
very little, and often no, water is required, especially
if mulching of some sort is put over the earth in
pots or boxes; but it should not be any material that
would harbor rats or mice. The leaves will fall
off, but this is not a danger signal, such plants being
deciduous in their natural climates. It will be best
to keep such plants as are to be stored in the cellar,
from the time there is danger of frost until about
November first, in an outbuilding or shed, where
they will not freeze. This makes the change more
gradual and natural. The temperature of the cellar should be as near thirty-four to thirty-eight degrees as possible. About March first will be time

to start giving most plants so treated heat, light
and water again, the latter gradually.

The fact that growth is made in advance of the
flowering period means that the summer care and
feeding of such plants is very important.   Plenty
of water must be given, and frequent applications
of liquid manure or fertilizers, or top dressing.
Flowering shrubs that bloom on last season's wood,
like hydrangeas, should be pruned just after blooming.

Abutilon—The   Flowering   Maple   (Abutilon)
is an old favorite, but well worthy of continued
popularity.   It is practically ever-blooming, which
at once marks it as highly desirable.   The pendulous flowers are very pretty, coming in shades of
pink, white, yellow and dark red.   The foliage is
also beautiful, especially that of the variegated varieties, than which very few plants are more worthy
of a place in the window gardener's collection.

New plants, which will grow and bloom very
rapidly, are propagated by cuttings rooted in the
fall or spring.   Give the plants when indoors plenty
of light.   Old plants, for which there is not room
in the window garden, may be wintered almost dry
in a cool place and allowing the leaves to fall off.

The varieties are numerous.   Some of the best
are Santana, deep red; Boule de Neige, pure white;
Gold Bell, yellow; *Darwini tesselatum;* Souvenir
de Bonn and Savitzii (the latter the most popular of

Grevillea robusta, the Silk Oak, is easily grown and an exceedingly graceful shrub for growing indoors

Otaheite orange. Their rest period should be given during
November, December and January

all variegated) ; Eclipse and vexillarium, trailing in habit.

Acalypha—Valuable for its variegated foliage. For use in the house root cuttings in early fall. The old roots, after cutting back, may be kept on the dry side to furnish cuttings in spring for the garden plants.

Aralia—Aralia *(Fatsia Japonica)* and *A. J. variegata,* especially the last, are two of the most decorative plants one may have. They are not widely known — very likely because they are difficult to propagate. Easily kept. Get from florist.

Ardisia—*(Ardisia crenulata)* is the best red berried plant for the house. It is a dwarf, with very beautiful dark green foliage. While kept healthy it will be laden constantly with its attractive clusters of berries, one crop lasting over the next. Seedlings make the best plants, and are readily grown. Sow in January to April, and plants will flower within a year and thereafter be perpetually decorated. Old plants can be topped (see page 86) and make fine specimens. By all means give the ardisia a place in your collection.

Aucuba—The Gold Dust Plant : one of the beautiful shrubs and especially valuable for decoration because doing well in such shaded positions as inner rooms, or by doorways. Strong tip cuttings — six to ten inches — can be rooted readily in the fall. Give a soil on the heavy side.

Azalea—The azalea is the most beautiful flowering shrub — if not the most beautiful of all winter flowering plants. With proper treatment an azalea should do service for several years, becoming more splendid each season.

You will probably get your plant when it is in full bloom. At this time, and during the whole growing season, it requires abundant water. The best way to make sure of giving it a thorough one, is to stand it for half an hour in a pail of water. Keep it in a rather cool place, say forty-five at night, and the flowering season, which should last several weeks, will be prolonged.

With the azaleas you must do the work for next year's success as soon as the flowering season is over. After repotting, keep in a temperature of fifty to fifty-five degrees at night.

There are three types of azalea suitable for winter blooming, the Indian, Ghent and Mollis, of each of which there are several kinds. The Indian type has the advantage of not blooming without its leaves, as the others do. The best way to select the varieties wanted is to purchase when in bloom. It will not pay the amateur to attempt propagation.

Bouvardia—Pink, white or red flowers, sweet scented. Propagated by root cuttings, but as the plants are good for a number of years, the best way is to get them from the florist. Old plants may be divided, small enough to go into number three pots. Give either cuttings or divisions about sixty degrees at night after potting, which should be in spring, until put outdoors. Keep pinched to shape. Then bloom from late fall to February.

Browallia—A very attractive flowering shrub, easily grown in a cool room, with plenty of sunlight. Sow seeds in 4-inch pots in August, thinning to three or four. Repot to 6 inches. Cuttings make good plants. Best grown as standards.

B. elata is especially valuable because of its deep blue flowers. *B. Jamesonii* is orange. Roezlii and Grandiflora, blue or white.

Daphne—*D. odora* is easily grown and very fragrant. As ornamental as orange or lemon and very free flowering. Give almost no water in winter, or store in cellar. Plants good for many years.

Genista—A beautiful evergreen shrub, bearing freely in spring clusters of pea-shaped yellow flowers, richly fragrant. Cut back after flowering, and in fall put in a cold room, forty degrees, or a frame, giving several weeks rest. Cuttings may be rooted readily in spring, when pruning the plants.

Grevillea robusta—The Silk Oak is grown with the greatest ease and makes an extremely graceful, beautiful plant, either by itself or as a center for fern dishes, etc. Sow in March and grow on with frequent shifts.

Hibiscus—One of the most brilliant flowering

shrubs outside of the azaleas, with single and double flowers.   Give a warm, sunny spot.   Large plants can be stored in the cellar.   Cuttings in spring or summer will furnish new plants.

Hydrangea—This is another popular flowering shrub, often had in bloom inside in the spring, but personally I do not consider it suited for such use. The flowers are rather coarse to bear close inspection, such as a house plant must be subject to: they are far more effective in masses out-of-doors or used as semi-formal decorations about paths or stoops, for which purpose they are unsurpassed.

If you care to have them bloom indoors, get small plants from the florist, or start cuttings of new growth in spring, taking shoots which do not have buds.   After flowering, cut back each branch and grow on, in a cool airy place with slight protection from noonday sun.   Take into the house before frost, and gradually dry off for a rest of six weeks or more in a cold room.   Then start into growth.

Plants for flowering early in the spring outdoors should be treated in the same way during summer, and wintered in the cellar, as directed above.   Take up to the light any time after first of March in the spring, but be careful to harden off before setting outside.

The varieties of the hydrangea are several, some being entirely hardy farther north than New York, but the sorts best for house and tub culture are not.

Most of them will come through some winters, but
it doesn't pay to take the chance.

H. Hortensia Japonica is the blue flowering variety; the color will depend much, however, upon the
soil. To make sure of the color, dissolve one pound
of alum in two quarts of ammonia, dilute with
twenty gallons water and use as a liquid fertilizer.
Thomas Hogg is a beautiful pure white, quite hardy.
H. h. Otaksa, pink, is one of the most popular.

Lantana—Easily grown flowering shrub, trailing
in habit, with small flower clusters of white, pink,
red, yellow or orange. New dwarf varieties best
for pot culture. Cuttings root easily. I have never
cared for this plant, and its odor is not pleasant to
most people.

Lemon—The best lemon for house culture is the
Ponderosa, or American Wonder, of comparatively
recent introduction. Most florists now have it.
Easily grown and a very attractive plant. The
fruit is good to use.

Lemon Verbena (Aloysia citriodora)—Many
people consider this the most delightfully fragrant
plant grown. Certainly no window garden should
be without it. Early in September cut back old
plants, if in the garden, and pot up. New growth
will quickly be made. Plants kept in pots should
be rested in early winter by keeping dry and cool.
Spring cuttings root easily.

Oleander—A beautiful old-time favorite, with

fragrant blossoms of red, pink, yellow or white.
Give a very rich soil and plenty of water when
growing. Rest after flowering. Cuttings are
rather hard, but will root with care.

Orange—There are several sorts suited to house
culture, and they should be more frequently tried,
as a well grown plant will have flowers, green fruit
and attractive golden oranges almost all the time —
to say nothing of its foliage beauty and delightful
fragrance. Their rest period should be given during November, December and January.

Otaheite Orange is the one most commonly
grown for house culture, and while the fruit is of
no use for eating, it has the more valuable advantage of remaining on the tree (which is eighteen to
twenty-four inches high) for months. Satsuma is
another good sort. Kumquat *(Citrus Japonica)* is
also very attractive.

*Reinwardtia (*known usually as *Linum trigynum)*
—Another attractive flowering shrub, with light or
bright yellow flowers. Cuttings will root with bottom heat in April. *L. tetragynum* is a companion
variety.

Roses—Those who will take the proper pains can
grow roses successfully in the house; but as a general rule satisfactory results are not obtained. The
first essential to success is the use of the right
varieties and those only. The second is a moist
atmosphere; the third is cleanliness,— insect enemies

must be kept off. For soils, growing in summer, etc., see Part II, page 188.

The best varieties for house culture are the Crimson Baby Rambler (Mme. Norbert Levavasseur), Pink Baby Rambler (Anchen Muller), Crimson Rambler, Clothilde Soupert, Agrippina, Hermosa, Safrano, Maman Cochet, White Maman Cochet and La France.

If the plants are set in a window-box (see page 9) about one foot apart, they will be more easily cared for than in pots. They may be treated in two ways. (1) After blooming, cut away most of the old growth and enforce rest during the summer. Start again in October and grow on in the house. (2) Grow on through the summer and dry off in the fall as the leaves drop. Store in a cold place (a little freezing will not hurt) until about January first. Then prune back severely — about half — and bring into warmth and water. A combination of the two methods will give a long flowering season.

Swainsona—A shrub of vine-like habit, bearing flowers, white and light pink, which greatly resemble sweet peas. The foliage is unusual and very pretty. It should be trained up to stakes or other supports and cut back quite severely after flowering.

Sweet Olive (Olea fragrans)—This is still another fragrant flowering shrub and one of the very easiest to grow.

The house shrubs, having harder stems and tougher leaves than other classes of plants, will stand many hardships that to the latter would prove fatal. They are, however, particularly susceptible to attacks of red spider and scale. *Keep your shrubs clean.* If you do not, in spite of their seeming immunity to harm, you will have no success with them. Syringing, showering, washing, spraying with insecticides, even giving a next-to-freezing rest, — all the remedies mentioned in Chapter XVII on Insects and Diseases — may at times have to be resorted to. But, at whatever trouble, if you want them at all, keep your shrubs clean.

Baby rambler rose. Few varieties of rose will stand the dry air and dust that oppress most house plants

Araucaria excelsa. Give little water in winter and a cool, even temperature

CHAPTER X

THE foliage plants depend very largely for their beauty upon making a rapid, unchecked growth and being given plenty of sunlight. In many of those having multi-colored and variegated leaves, the markings under unfavorable conditions of growth become inconspicuous and the value of the plant is entirely lost. Therefore, where the proper conditions cannot be given, it will be far wiser to devote your space to plants more suited to house culture.

Aspidistra, araucaria, Pandanus and the rubber plant are exceptions; two of them being remarkable for their hardihood under neglect and ignornce. While many of the foliage plants will live under almost any conditions, it must be remembered, however, that the better care they receive the more beautiful they will be.

Achyranthes—Achyranthes are still popular as bedding plants, as they furnish good coloring. They may be used as house plants also, but in my opinion are a little coarse. Take cuttings in August for new plants and keep on the warm side and rather dry in winter.

Alternanthera—These little plants are unique and brilliant, and a few will be worth having in any collection. They make dense, shrubby miniature bushes a few inches high, very attractively colored. Take cuttings in August; give rich soil, on the sandy side, plenty of light and heat.

A. versicolor has leaves bearing a happy contrast of pink, crimson and bronzy-green. *Tricolor* is dark green, rose and orange. There are numerous other attractive varieties.

Anthericum (A. variegatum) — The foliage is shaped like a broad blade of grass and very prettily bordered with white. Of the easiest culture, doing well in the shade. Propagated by division. *A. medio-picta* is another variety, often considered more attractive than the above.

Araucaria—The several araucarias should be much more widely known than they are. Their beauty has made them popular as Christmas gifts, but most of the fine specimens which leave the florists during the holiday season find their end, after a few weeks in a gas-tainted, superheated atmosphere, with probably several times the amount of water required given at the roots, in the ash barrel. They are, when one knows something of their habits of growth, very easily cared for. Little water in winter, and a cool even temperature, are its simple requirements.

The araucaria is, I think, the most beautiful of

all formal decorative plants.   Its dignity, simplicity
and beautiful plumelike foliage place it in a class of
its own.   The branches leave the main stem at regular intervals, in whorls of five, and the foliage is a
clean soft green, lighter at the tips.   Propagated by
cuttings from leading shoots, not side shoots.

The two varieties ordinarily used are *A. excelsa
glauca* and *A. e. robusta*.   Some time ago I saw
a specimen of a new variety, not yet put on the
market, and the name of which I have forgotten.
(I think it was *stellata*)   The outer half of each
branch was almost white, giving the whole plant a
wonderful star-like effect.

Aspidistra—The aspidistra is the toughest
of all foliage plants — if not of all house plants.   It
has proved hardy out-of-doors as far north as
Philadelphia.   The long flat leaves grow to a height
of eighteen to twenty-four inches, springing directly
from the ground.   Its chief requirement is plenty of
water during the growing season.   New plants are
readily obtained by dividing the old roots in February or August.

There are several varieties and those familiar only
with the common green sort (*A. elatior*) will be
surprised and pleased with the striking effective-
ness of the variegated, (*A. e. varigata*) and with
the spotted leaved *A. punctata*.

Caladium—This is another popular plant for
which I have never cared greatly myself.   It seems

to have no personality. Well grown plants, however, give most gorgeous color effects. Buy bulbs
of the fancy-leaved section, and start in February or
March, giving very little water at first. Take in
before the first sign of frosts. When growth stops,
dry off gradually and store in warm cellar; or better,
take out of pots and pack in sand. Do not let them
dry out enough to shrivel.

Coleus—The best of all the gay colored foliage
plants, but tender. To keep looking well in winter
they must have plenty of warmth and sunlight.
Root cuttings in August. They grow on very rapidly. Make selections from the garden or a florist's,
as they come in a great variety of colors and markings.

Dracæna—The best of all plants, outside the
palms, for centers of vases, boxes and large pots.
Small plants make very beautiful centers for fern
dishes. The colored section need to be kept on the
warm side. Give plenty of water in summer, but
none on the leaves in winter, as it is apt to lodge in
the leaf axils and cause trouble.

Dracæna (Cordyline)—*Indivisa,* with long, narrow, recurved green leaves, is the one mostly used.
The various colored sorts are described in most
catalogues.

Leopard Plant—*Farfugium grande,* better known
as Leopard Plant, has handsome dark green leaves
marked with yellow. It is of the easiest culture,

standing zero weather. Old plants may be divided
in spring and rooted in sand. There is a newer
variety with white spots, very beautiful. The farfugium is now more commonly listed as *Senecio
Kaempferi.*

Pandanus—The Screw Pine is another favorite decorative plant, easily grown. The leaves
are two or three feet long and come out spirally, as
the name indicates. As they get older they curve
down gracefully, giving a very pleasing effect.

The soil for pandanuses should contain a generous amount of sand. Give plenty of water in summer, little in winter, and be sure that none of it
lodges in the axils of the leaves, as rot is very easily
induced.

New plants are produced from suckers at the
base of the old ones.

Pandanus utilis is the variety most commonly
seen. *P. Veitchii,* dark green bordered with broad
stripes of pure white, is much more decorative, a
really beautiful plant. *P. Sanderi* is another good
sort, with golden yellow coloring, that should be
given a trial.

Pepper.—Some of the peppers make very attractive pot plants on account of their bright fruit, which
is very pretty in all stages of growth from the new
green pods, through yellow to bright red. Buy new
plants or start from seed in spring. They are
easily grown if kept on the warm side. Celestial

and Kaleidoscope are the two kinds best suited for house culture.

The Rubber (*Ficus.*)   This is the most popular of all formal decorative plants.   At least part of the secret of its success undoubtedly lies in the fact that — almost literally — you cannot kill it! But that is no excuse for abusing it either, as there is all the difference in the world between a well cared for symmetrical plant and one of the semi-denuded, lop-sided, spotted leaved plants one so frequently sees, and than which, as far as ornamentation is concerned, an empty pot would be far more decorative.

The rubber requires — and deserves — a good rich soil, and in the spring, summer and fall, all the water that the soil will keep absorbed.   Give less in winter, as an excess at this time causes the leaves to turn yellow and droop.

As the rubber is more difficult to propagate than most house plants, and specimens will not get too large for several years, it will be best to get plants from the florist.   It frequently happens, however, that an old plant which has been grown up to a single stem, becomes unwieldy, and bare at the bottom.   In such cases the upper part may be removed by " topping " and the main trunk cut back to within six to eighteen inches of the pot or tub, and water withheld partly until new growth starts. The old stem may thus be transformed into a low,

bush plant and frequently they make very handsome specimens.   The topping is performed by making a deep upward slanting cut, with a sharp knife,
at the point you want in the pot for your new plant.
In the cut stuff a little sphagnum moss; remove this
after a few days and wash the cut out with warm
water, removing the congealed sap.   Insert fresh
moss and with strips of soft cloth tie a good hand-
ful over the wound.   *Keep this moist* constantly
until the roots show through the moss, which may
be several weeks.   Then pot in *moist* earth, not
wet, and syringe daily, but do not water the pots
for two or three days.   Sometimes pots cut in
halves and the bottoms partly removed are used to
hold the moss in place.   August is a good time to
propagate.

Ficus elastica is the common rubber plant.   The
" fiddle-leaved " rubber plant (*F. pandurata*) is another variety, now largely grown.   It differs from
the former in having very broad, blunt leaves,
shaped like the head of a fiddle, which are marked
by the whitish veins.   Two other beautiful plants
are *F. Cooperia,* having large leaves with red mid-
ribs, and *F. Parcelli,* with leaves marbled with
white.   They should be given a higher temperature
than *F. elastica.*

Saxifraga: S. sarmentosa tricolor is the commonly
known strawberry geranium, or beefsteak plant.   It
has a quite unique habit of growth and is best dis-

played where its numerous runners have a chance to hang down, as from a basket or hanging pot. The runners are easily rooted in soil. There are numerous varieties, with flowers of red, white and pink.

Sensitive Plant (Mimosa pudica)—This is a pretty little green-leaved plant, the never-failing interest in which lies not in its beauty, however, but in the fact that it shrinks and folds up when touched, as though it belonged to the animal kingdom. It is easily grown from seed.

Tradescantia—This is otherwise known as spiderwort, Wandering Jew, Creeping Charles and under other names. It is a very pretty running or trailing plant, of the easiest culture, its chief requirement being plenty of water. Cuttings root easily at any time. There are several varieties, among them being *discolor*, a variegated leaf, and *Zebrina multicolor*, the leaves of which give almost a rainbow effect in their wonderful diversity and blending. For those familiar only with the old green variety it will prove a great surprise.

Zebra Plant (Maranta zebrina)—This is another easily grown decorative plant with tropical looking, large leaves. While usually listed as *Maranta zebrina*, it is really a calathea and the plants of this genus show a variation in their markings unsurpassed by any. Zebrina and most of the varieties, of which there are many, should be grown in the shade, with plenty of water and a minimum temper-

Pandanus Veitchii, the Screw Pine. The soil for this family should have a generous amount of sand

The rubber plant (*Ficus elastica*), perhaps the most popular of all formal decorative house plants

ature of sixty degrees all the year. *C. pulchella* and *C. intermedia* resembles *C. zebrina* and can be grown in a cooler temperature. Do not allow the plants to flower. Increase by division.

CHAPTER XI

A NUMBER of the vines make very excellent house plants, though one seldom sees them. This seems rather strange when one takes into consideration the facts that they are easily grown and can be used for decorative effects impossible with any other plants.

If there is one particular caution to be given in regard to caring for plants in the house, it is to *keep the foliage clean*. Naturally a vine that runs up the window trim, and maybe halfway across the wall to a picture frame, cannot well be sprinkled or syringed; but the leaves can be occasionally wiped off with a moist, soft cloth. Keep the pores open; they have to breathe.

Cissus discolor—This altogether too little known vine has the most beautiful foliage of any. The leaves are a velvety green veined with silver, the under surfaces being reddish and the stems red. It is a rapid grower and readily managed if kept on the warm side. New plants may be had from cuttings at almost any season. *C. antarctica* is better known and easily grown.

Clematis—This popular outdoor vine is some-

times successfully used as a house plant, and has
the advantage of doing well in a low temperature.
Cuttings rooted in June and grown on will make
good plants, but the best way will be to get at the
florist's two or three plants of the splendid new
varieties now to be had.

Cobœa scandens—The cobœa is sometimes called
the cup-and-saucer flower. It is very energetic,
growing under good conditions to a length of twenty
to thirty feet. The flowers, which are frequently
two inches across, are purplish in color and very
pretty. They are borne quite freely.

The cobœa is easily managed if kept properly
trained. As the plant in proportion to the pot room
is very large, liquid manures or fertilizers are desirable. Either seeds or cuttings will furnish new
plants. The former should be placed edge down,
one in a two-inch pot and pressed in level with the
surface. They will soon need repotting, and must
be shifted frequently until they are put in six- or
eight-inch pots.

Cobœa scandens variegata is a very handsome
form and should without fail be tried.

Hoya carnosa—This is commonly known as the
wax plant on account of its thick leaves and wax-
like flowers, which are a delicate pink and borne in
large pendulous umbels. It is easily cared for; give
full sun in summer and keep moderately dry in
winter. Leave the old flower stalks on the plant.

Cuttings may be rooted in early spring in pots, plunged in bottom heat.

The Ivys—The ivys are the most graceful of all the vines, and with them the most artistic effects in decoration may be produced. I have always wondered why they are not more frequently used, for they are in many respects ideal as house plants; they produce more growth to a given size pot than any other plants, they thrive in the shade, they withstand the uncongenial conditions usually found in the house, and are among the hardiest of plants suitable for house culture. And yet how many women will fret and fume over a Lorraine begonia or some other refractory plant, not adapted at all to growing indoors, when half the amount of care spent on a few ivys would grace their windows with frames of living green, giving a setting to all their other plants which would enhance their beauty a hundred percent.

The English ivy (*Hedera helix*) is the best for house culture. A form with small leaves, *H. Donerailensis,* is better for many purposes. And then there is a variegated form, which is very beautiful. Large cuttings, rooted in the fall, will make good plants. *Hedera helix arborescens* is known as the Irish ivy and is a very rapid grower.

The German ivy (*Senecio scandens*) has leaves the shape of the English ivy, and is a wonderfully rapid grower and a great climber. It lacks, how-

ever, the substance and coloring of the real ivy.
It is, nevertheless, valuable for temporary uses, and
a plant or two should always be kept.   Cuttings
root freely and grow at any time.

Manettia—This is a cheery, free flowering little
vine, especially good for covering a small trellis in a
pot.   The brilliant little flowers, white, blue or red
and yellow, are very welcome winter visitors.   Cuttings root easily in summer and the plants are very
easily cared for, being particularly free from insect
pests.   Give partial shade in summer.

Mimosa   moschatus—This   is   the   common
Musk Plant which, according to one's taste, is pleasant — or the opposite.   It is of creeping habit and
has very pretty foliage.

There are a number of varieties.   That described
above is covered with small yellow flowers.   *M. m.
Harrisonii* has larger flowers.   *M. cardinalis,* red
flowers and is dwarf in habit.   *M. glutinosus* is
erect in habit, with salmon colored flowers, very
pretty.

Moneywort   (Lysimachia   Nummularia)—This
is a favorite basket plant, as it is a rapid grower and
not particular about its surroundings, so long as
it has enough water.   While the flowers are pretty,
being a cheery yellow, the plant is grown for its
foliage.   New plants may be had by dividing old
clumps.

Morning-Glory—This beautiful flower is seldom

seen in the house, but will do well there if plenty of light can be given.   Neither vines nor flowers grow as large as they do out-of-doors, but they make very pretty plants.

Nasturtium—Another common summer flower that makes a very pretty plant in the house.   Start seeds in August and shift on to five-or-six-inch pots. There is also a dwarf form and other sorts with variegated ivy leaves that make splendid pot plants. Of the tall sorts some of the new named varieties, like Sunlight and Moonlight, give beautiful and very harmonious effects.   They will be a very pleasant surprise to those familiar only with the old bright mixed colors.

Othonna crassifolia—This pretty little yellow flowered trailing plant, sometimes known as " little Pickles " is quite a favorite for boxes, or as a hanging or bracket plant.   It should be given the full sun but little water in winter.   When too long, it it may be cut back freely.   Root cuttings, or the small tufts along the trailing stems, in spring.

Smilax—In some ways this is the most airily beautiful and graceful of all the decorative vines. And it is valuable not only for its own beauty, but for its usefulness in setting off the beauty of other flowers.   It is very easily grown if kept on the warm side, and given plenty of root room.   Care should be taken to provide green colored strings for the vines to climb up, as they make a very rapid

growth when once started. The best way to provide plants is to get a few from the florist late in
the spring, or start from seed in February. New
plants do better than those kept two seasons.

Sweet Peas—Of late years a great deal has been
done with sweet peas in winter, and where one can
give them plenty of light, they will do well inside.
Plenty of air and a temperature a little
on the cool side, with rich soil, will suit them.
Start seed in very early fall, or in winter, according as you want bloom early or late. There are
now a number of varieties grown especially for
winter work such as Christmas Pink, Christmas
White, etc. Five or six varieties will give a very
satisfactory collection. The fragrant, beautiful
blossoms are always welcome, but doubly so in winter. Do not let the flowers fade on the vines, as it
increases the number of flowers to have them taken
off.

Thunbergia—The Thunbergia, sometimes called
the " butterfly plant," is the best all-round flowering
vine for the house. The flowers are freely produced, average an inch to an inch-and-a-half across,
and cover a wide range of colors, including white,
blue, purple, yellow and shades and combinations
of these. Its requirements are not special: keep
growing on during summer into a somewhat bushy
form, as the vines will grow rapidly when allowed
to run in the house. It can be grown from seed

but cuttings make the best plants.   Root early in spring, and by having a succession of rooted cuttings blossoms may be had all winter.

Thunbergia laurifolia has flowers of white and blue; *T. fragrans,* pure white; and *T. Mysorensis,* purple and yellow.

One too seldom sees vines used indoors, although they are
easily grown and can be made most decorative

The Crested Scott Fern (*Nephrolepis exaltata*, var. *Scholzeli*) is one of the most beautiful developments from the Boston Fern

CHAPTER XII

FERNS, although there are not many varieties of them available for culture indoors, are probably more universally used as house plants than any other class of plants. Their culture is not difficult, although it differs somewhat from that given most of the plants described in the preceding pages.

In the first place, ferns want a porous soil, say two parts screened leaf-mould, one sand and one old manure or rich loam, the latter being preferable. In the second place, they should be given a warmer temperature, a minimum of fifty-five degrees at night being very desirable, although not absolutely essential.

The third requisite in success with ferns is a moist atmosphere, as well as plenty of water at the roots. If the pots are carefully drained (facing page 41) as they should be, and the soil properly porous, it will be almost impossible to over-water at the roots. Great care should be taken, however, not to wet the foliage, particularly where the sun can shine on the leaves. When the fronds must be wet, to keep them clean, try to do it on a warm day, that they may dry off quickly near an open north or east window. They should always be given as much light as possible, without direct sunlight, and as much air as possible while maintaining the proper temperature.

Many of the ferns can be increased either by runners or division, and these are easily propagated at home. Those which are grown from spores (the fern's seeds) it will be better to get from the florist's.

Most of the ferns belong to one of three groups, the sword ferns (*Nephrolepis*), the maidenhairs (*Adiantum*) or the spider ferns (*Pteris*). The distinguishing feature of the sword ferns is their long pointed fronds; the maidenhairs command attention by their beautiful feathery foliage, in some varieties as delicate as the filmiest lace; and the spider ferns, seen usually in mixed varieties in dishes or fern pans, are attractive for their shades of green, gray, white and silver, and compact growth.

THE SWORD FERNS

The old widely popular sword fern was *Nephrolepis exaltata,* but the original form has been almost entirely replaced by new varieties developed from it, the most widely known of which is the Boston fern (*N. ex. var. Bostoniensis*). The wide popularity of this fern is due to both its beauty and its hardiness, as it will stand more ill usage than any other house fern. It grows rapidly and makes a handsome plant at all stages of development.

THE SCOTT FERN

A well grown large Boston fern requires a good deal of room, and the long fronds — three feet or more in length — are apt to get damaged at the ends. For these reasons the *Scottii* fern, a development of the Boston, is for some purposes a better plant. Its fronds are like those of the latter, but shorter and proportionately narrower, and the habit of the plant is much more dense and compact. It makes a very satisfactory plant.

THE PLUMED TYPE

Another fern developed from the Boston is *Whitmani,* in which the fronds are not so long but the foliage is so finely divided that it gives a decided plumey effect. The *Whitmani* is perhaps the best of this type for house culture as the others, under adverse conditions, are likely to revert to the Boston type of frond. *Piersoni* and *Elegantissima* are exceptionally beautiful, but must be given careful attention. *Scholzeli,* sometimes called the Crested Scott fern, is very beautiful and well worth trying.

THE MAIDENHAIRS

Of the beautiful, but delicate, adiantums perhaps the one most frequently seen in the florist's window is *A. Farleyense,* with its drooping, lace-like, light green leaves. It is not, however, suited for house

culture and while it can be made to succeed, do not
waste time in trying it until you have mastered the
growing of the hardier sorts.

However, just because *Farleyense* is so delicate,
do not feel that you cannot have any maidenhair
fern.   *Croweanum* is another beautiful adiantum,
and as its fronds are much firmer than those of most
of this class, it withstands the trying conditions of
house culture very satisfactorily.   Another maidenhair, often called the hardy *Farleyense,* is *Adiantum
c. v. imbricatum.*   As its name suggests, it looks
very much like the Farley fern, but it is suitable for
house culture.   It is a very satisfactory fern.   And
just recently there is another from England called
the Glory fern (Glory of Moordrecht).   I have not
seen it, but certainly from photographs and what the
horticultural journals have said of it, it will make a
very fine fern for the winter garden.

THE SPIDER FERNS

The name given *Pteris* ferns is descriptive of only
part of them, as they vary greatly.   They are commonly used in made up dishes, or with other plants,
but most of them will make fine single plants as well.
P. Wilsoni is a popular sort making a compact plant
with a unique tufted foliage of light clear green.
P. cretica is dark green, or green lined with white,
according to the variety.   *Victoriæ* is perhaps the
best of the several variegated Pteris'.

The Boston Fern is easily propagated at home by division

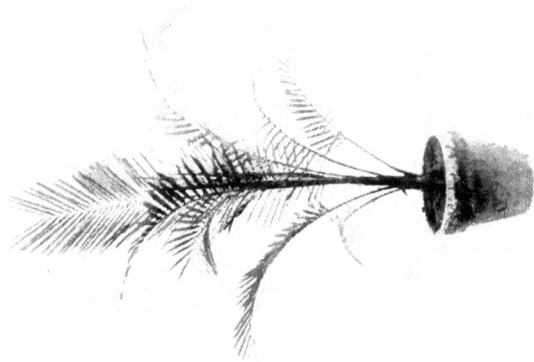

Cocus Weddelliana is a small palm but one of the most graceful of all

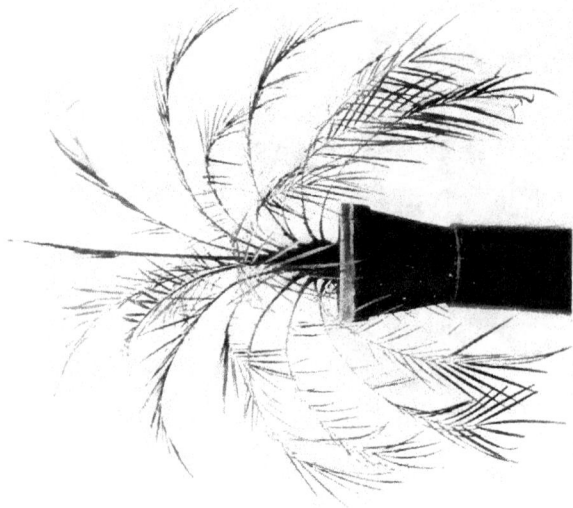

Phoenix Roebelenii is one of the more recent and best developments of the old favorite Fan Palms

OTHER FERNS

The Holly fern *(Cyrtomium falcatum)* is another
very desirable house plant and has been a favorite
for years.   It has very dark green substantial glossy
foliage, and stands up well.   There is a new Holly
fern, however, which I think will replace *C. falcatum;* it is *C. Rochfordianum;* its foliage is not
only a richer deeper green, but the pinnae, or leaf-
lets, are deeply cut and also wavy, and have given
it the popular name of the Crested Holly fern.   Be
sure to try it among the next ferns you get.

Fern balls, which are usually composed of one of
the *Davallias,* sometimes prove unsatisfactory.   Be
sure in ordering to get them fresh from some reliable mail order house, rather than take chances
on them at the florist's.   The best way, however,
is to get them already started.   If you get them in
dormant condition, soak in tepid water and then
give a temperature as near sixty degrees at night as
possible until they start.

While not strictly members of the fern family,
the asparagus used for decorative purposes under
the name of Asparagus Ferns, are commonly classed
with them.   Since their introduction they have
proved very popular indeed.

Asparagus plumosus nanus, the Lace fern.   No
foliage is more beautiful than the feathery light
green sprays of this asparagus.   Notwithstanding
its delicacy, it keeps wonderfully well when cut.

The plants can be grown as pot plants, or as vines.
If wanted for the former purpose, keep the sprays
pinched back at twelve inches, and the roots rather
restricted.   For vines, keep in large pots or boxes
— always well drained — and keep well fed.

Asparagus Sprengeri in both foliage and habit is
very distinct from *A. plumosus.*   The leaves resemble small glossy pine needles, borne in long
sprays, and as it is trailing in habit it makes a unique
and beautiful plant for stands or baskets.   The
sprays keep well when cut, and make an excellent
background for flowers.   It is now used more universally for green by florists than any other plant.

Either of the above may be started from seed, or
propagated by dividing old plants, but small young
plants may be had of the florists at a very low price.
They need about the same treatment as smilax (see
page 94), but will do well in a temperature of fifty
to fifty-five degrees at night.   Shower frequently,
but water only moderately.

For many years these two varieties have held the
field to themselves, but recently a new asparagus,
of each type has put in an appearance.   *Hatcheri* resembles *plumosus nanus,* but is more compact in
habit and the leaves are much closer together on the
stems.   If it remains true to type, and is as hardy as
plumosus, it will replace it, for it certainly is a more
beautiful plant.   *A. S. variegata* is a very pretty
" sport " with the leaves edged white.

CHAPTER XIII

PALMS

THE number of palms adapted to house culture is very limited but they comprise the most elegant of the decorative plants.

Although popular now, they would be much more widely used if their culture were better understood. Mistakes made in handling palms are serious in results, for they produce for the most part only two or three new leaves in a year, and so any injury shows for a long time; it is not soon replaced by new growth and forgotten, as with many of the more rapid growing house plants.

Nevertheless, if the few cultural requirements of palms are carefully attended to, they are as easily grown as any plants and yield a solid and lasting satisfaction.

The house palms, as I have said, grow very slowly. It is not only useless, but dangerous, to try to force them into unnatural growth.

Palms do best when restricted as to root room. When your plant comes from the florist, do not get impatient after a month or so and think that a larger pot would make it grow faster. Repotting once a year while palms are growing, and not so frequently

as that after they are in eight- or ten-inch pots, will
be sufficient. The best time for repotting is late
spring — May or June. Use a pot only one size
larger than that in which the palm has been growing.
Remove carefully, *do not disturb the roots,* and put
into the new pot carefully, ramming the new earth
in firmly about the old ball with a thin piece of
wood (see directions for repotting, page 40).

The soil for palms need not contain as much
humus (leaf-mould or peat) as that for most other
house plants. Good rich garden loam, with sharp
sand added, and bone meal worked through it, will
be right.

Be sure the drainage is perfect. Crock the pots
carefully (facing page 41). If any of the crocking
from the old pot comes out with the ball of earth,
remove it as carefully as possible and fill in the space
with soil. After potting, keep shaded for several
days.

While palms require plenty of water, no plants
are more fatally injured by overwatering. Above
all must care be taken never to let water accumulate
in saucers or jardinieres in which the pots are standing. Water will soak up through a pot as well as
down through it, and water-saturated soil will
quickly become sour. When you do water, water
thoroughly and then see that the pots are kept where
they can drain out, and do not water again until
they show a tendency to get too dry. Much water

will cause the leaves to turn brown. In this case change the treatment at once. (The looks of the leaves can be somewhat improved by cutting them to shape with a pair of scissors.) The amount of water required is much greater in summer than in winter, when the plants are practically at rest.

Direct sunlight is not desirable for palms, but they should have plenty of light. Do not stick them away in a dark corner or an inner room and expect them to do well. They will stand such a situation several days without injury, but should be brought back to the light as soon as possible. They do well in north windows, providing the temperature of the room is high enough. Remember, however, that pots kept in a shady place will dry out much less quickly than those in the light or sunlight. If they are to be kept permanently where the sun does not strike, it is a good thing to add charcoal to the soil, as this aids greatly in keeping it from getting sour.

Give plenty of air. The more the better, so long as a proper temperature is kept up, as that counteracts the effect of the more or less poisonous atmosphere of living-rooms kept closed during winter. Beware of drafts blowing across the plants, but provide plenty of fresh air.

In the spring as soon as it warms up outdoors — say after the apple blossoms fall — plunge the palms outside, in a sheltered position, where they

can be given plenty of water. At this time, if they
are not repotted, bone meal should be worked into
the surface of the soil and a liquid manure of bone
meal given once a month or so during the growing
season.

Both during winter and summer, *shower the
leaves frequently,* with as forceful a stream as possible, to prevent scale and mealy-bug getting a start.
(For treatment see page 135.) Keep the leaves and
stems clean by wiping off every once in a while with
a soft cloth and soapy warm water, syringing with
clean water afterwards.

THE BEST HOUSE PALMS

Although the number of palms cultivated is very
large, very few indeed — only about a dozen — will
give satisfactory results in the house. The fact that
a palm will live — or rather, takes a very long time
to die — under abuse, has misled people into thinking that they do not need as much care as other
house plants. This is a mistake.

Palms may be considered in two classes, the fan-
leaved and the feather-leaved, or deeply cut, sorts.
Of the former there are but three sorts good for
house culture.

Latania Borbonica, the Chinese Fan-leaved palm,
is the best known. It is one of the hardiest, standing a temperature as low as forty-five degrees at
night. It is broad in habit, and the large leaves are

deeply cut and drooping at the edge, making a very attractive plant.

Livistona rotundifolia, the Miniature Fan palm, is a more compact type of the above; not only the leaves but the whole plant being round in habit and growing quite dense.   It is a beautiful lively green in color, and making a neater plant, is in many ways more desirable for the house than *Latania Bor-bonica.*   It requires more warmth, however, and should be kept up to 55 degrees at night if possible.

Chamærops excelsa has the distinguished feature of forming shoots at the base, thus having foliage where most palms are bare, and in old specimens un-attractively so.   Its leaves are shaped like those of *Borbonica,* but are smaller, and the leaf stalk in pro-portion is longer.   It is a good strong variety.

THE FEATHER-LEAVED PALMS

Many of these are of more recent introduction than the old favorite fan palms, but they have won their way to a growing and deserved popularity.

Phoenix Rœbelenii is one of the newest.   It is destined, I venture to say, to become the most pop-ular of all palms for the house.   It has frequently been described as having "the beauty of *Weddel-liana* and the hardiness of *Kentia.*"   That perhaps describes it, but does not do it full justice.   It has several times the amount of foliage that *Cocos Wed-delliana* has, and is a more robust grower.   It has, unlike that palm, leaf stalks growing all the way to the bottom, the lower ones gracefully recurved and the upper ones spreading airily. It is very easily cared for, and on the whole wins on a larger number of counts than any other house palm.

Phoenix Rupicola has gracefully arching, drooping foliage and is very handsome, the dark green leaves being even more feather-like than those of *Cocus Weddelliana*. It is also one of the hardiest.

Areca Verschaffeltii is unique in having a creamy colored mid-rib. It must be given the best of care, but will well repay any extra pains taken with it.

The *Kentias, K. Belmoreana,* the Thatch-leaf palm, and *K. Forsteriana,* the Curly palm, are the hardiest of all the house palms and sure to give satisfaction. The former is of dwarf, sturdy habit, with broadly divided, dark green leaves borne up well on stiff stems. *K. Forsteriana* is of stronger growth, spreads more, and the divisions of the leaf are broader.

Cocos Weddelliana is the most artistically graceful of the house palms. The finely cut, feathery leaves spring well up from the pot and from the slender erect stem. It is a small palm, and grows slowly. I think I should give it a place among the three choicest palms for the house, although, unfortunately, it is not as hardy as some of the others. It is the best palm to use as a center for fern dishes.

Seaforthia elegans, the Australian Feather palm,

is a tall growing and stately variety, which does well in the house.

Caryota urens is commonly known as the Fish-tail palm, and on account of that distinguishing characteristic deserves a place in any good collection. It is a large growing sort and will utilize more root room than most of the others. It is not so strong as most of the others described, but will succeed well if precautions are taken not to let it get chilled in cold weather.

CHAPTER XIV

CACTI

PERSONALLY I am not an enthusiast over cacti. While a cactus in bloom is a marvelous sight, so gorgeous in fact that it is almost unbelievable and unreal, I prefer flowers a little less fervid and more constant.

There are, however, two distinct advantages which most of the cacti possess, making them available for use where no other plants could be kept. They are practically proof against any hardships that may be imposed upon them, and they take up very little room. In addition to that they are always an interesting curiosity, and for that reason alone well worth the little attention they require. The low-growing sorts, among which some of the most curious are to be found, may be given a narrow shelf or the edge of the plant shelf in the winter window garden.

As far as care and soil are concerned, their requirements are simple. The most important thing to see to is that they are given perfect drainage. The soil should be sandy, and coal ashes, or better still, old plastering or lime rubbish, should be added. Only a moderate amount of water will be required

in winter, but when the plants are set outside in a
well drained position in summer they should be
showered frequently. As to temperature, although
they come from hot climates, most of the sorts will
stand as low as thirty-five degrees without injury.
Just before and during the blooming period about
sixty degrees is desirable, but forty-five to fifty
degrees will be better at other times. Where room
is lacking, they may, for the most part, be wintered
over in the cellar, as described previously for other
plants (page 71). Propagation is performed either
by seeds or cuttings, the latter being the more generally used, as they root very readily — just break
a piece off and stick it in the sand.

Considered from the layman's point of view, cacti
are made up of two classes: those which are valued
for their wonderful flowers and those which excite
curiosity by their weird habits of growth. Some
of the latter — such as the Crown of Thorns and
the *Mammillaria* — have small or infrequent flowers.

Specimens of this class, well cared for, are worthy
of a place in any collection of flowering plants.
They will stand, especially during the flowering
period, weak applications of manure water.

The *Epiphyllums* or Crab cacti *(Ephiphyllum
truncatum* and its varieties) are by far the most
valuable, because of their profuse and long flowering season, especially as it comes in the winter when
bright flowers are scarce. *E. t. coccineum,* with

deep scarlet flowers, is one of the best. *Rucker-
ianum,* light purple with violet center; *Magni-
ficum,* white, slightly pinkish at the edge; and *vio-
laceum superbum,* white with rich purple edge, are
some of the other good varieties of these beautiful
plants. *Phyllocactus* is perhaps the next best
flowering sort. The flowers are larger, more gorgeous, but borne only for a very short time. *P. Ack-
ermanni* is one of the best of these. It has very
large flowers, lily-shaped, bright red shading to light
red with the inner petals, and the long gracefully
curved stamens add to its beauty. It blossoms in
May or early June, but the season is usually limited
to two or three weeks. The night blooming *Phyllocactus,* with white flowers, is commonly confused
with the Night-Blooming cereus. Cereus may be
distinguished by its angular stems as compared to
the broad flat stems of *Phyllocactus. C. grandi-
florus* and *C. Macdonaldiae,* the famous Night-
blooming cereuses, have white flowers which remain
open only one night. They are, however, though so
transient, a marvelous sight. Prone to strange tasks
indeed is the hand of Nature which has fashioned
these grotesque, clumsy, lifeless looking plants to
accumulate nourishment and moisture for months
from the niggardly desert sands, and to mature for
a few hours' existence only these marvelously fashioned flowers which collapse with the first rays of
the heat-giving sunshine. *C. flagelliformis,* and

C. speciosissimus, two very gorgeous flowered day blooming sorts, remain longer, but they are not so hardy as most of the other cacti. *Opuntia,* the Indian fig, is another flowering sort, though not so valuable. They are grotesque in shape and the flowers, which are various shades of red or yellow and two inches or so across, according to variety, look as though they had been stuck onto the plant.

Of the other cacti commonly grown most are of dwarf form and a single window will accommodate quite a number of them.

Echinocactus, the Hedge-hog cactus, is one of the best known of these. *E. myriostigma,* the Bishop's Cap, is a quite familiar variety.

Echinopsis, the Sea-urchin cactus, is another queer dwarf type. The flowers seem much too large for the plants, being sometimes half a foot long. They are lily-shaped and rose pink or white, according to variety.

Pilocereus senilis, the Old Man cactus, is another sort which always attracts attention in any collection. The stem is covered with fine white hairy spines, three to five inches long, which give it a very peculiar appearance. When kept in the house the hairs are likely to become dusty and grimy. They may be protected by cutting two panes of glass into four long pieces, just wide enough to square the pot, and enclosing it, putting a fifth piece over the top.

Opuntia senilis, the dwarf prickly pear, is very similar to the above, but indoors makes a larger plant usually, although much smaller in its natural habitat.

Anhalonium fissuratum, the Living Rock, is another frequently encountered and very interesting sort.

The *Mammillarias* are compact, neat little plants quite unique and attractive in spite of their spiral rows of vicious spines. They grow only a few inches high and have inconspicuous pale flowers of yellow, red or purple, followed by the bright red little fruits which are one of the most interesting characteristics. *M. bicolor* is one of the best and most frequently encountered sorts. *M. plumosa* has fuzzy spines, like the Old Man cactus. It can be kept clean by growing under a large glass.

There are several succulent plants quite closely resembling cacti, which need about the same treatment.

The century plant *(Agave Americana)* is universally known. There are two sorts frequently seen, that with the green leaves and a variety with broad yellow bands which is much handsomer. They make excellent formal tub plants, standing almost any hardships and lasting for years. They are easily propagated from suckers and grow quite rapidly. They are, however, in the larger sizes very difficult to handle, armed with spines at leaf tips

and edges. Tub specimens are usually wintered
over in the cellar, or at the florist's. There is an
unfounded superstition that they bloom once every
hundred years. They rarely flower when domesti-
cated. Repot as often as needed, in fairly rich soil,
while growing. Small plants are quite attractive in
the house in winter and may be plunged outside in
summer. The Crown of Thorns *(Euphorbia
splendens)* is also quite well known. It makes a long
tangled vine, full of wicked short thorns and small,
pretty leaves. The flowers are not large but the
bright red bracts add a touch of color and the plant
is covered with them most of the year. It must be
carefully staked up and trained, a short wide pot
trellis being the best thing to use.

"Little Pickles" *(Othonna crassifolia)* is quite
a favorite basket and hanging plant. The odd,
thick foliage looks like small cucumbers. It must
be given plenty of light, sunshine if possible, to
produce its flowers, which are small and yellow, in
shape like those of the sun pink, but smaller.

There are a number of other succulents sometimes
used for house plants, among them the aloes, mesem-
bryanthemums (fig marigolds), echeverias (*E.
metallica* being the best sort), sedums and house
leeks *(Sempervivums)*, among which *S. globifcrum,*
"hen-and-chickens," is the most widely known.
These do not occupy very important positions, however, and space does not permit further description
here.

CHAPTER XV

BULBS furnish one of the most satisfactory classes of winter-blooming house plants, especially for city houses and apartments where conditions are not apt to favor the longevity of plants.

They may be considered in two classes: — the forcing bulbs, such as narcissus and freesia, and those given natural conditions of growth in pots, such as amaryllis or callas.

Most of the forcing bulbs are included in what florists term the "Dutch" and "Cape" bulbs. They may be had in a succession of bloom from Thanksgiving to Easter, and yet all the work is done at one time. The task of bringing them to bloom is an easy one.

If you want to have the enjoyment of attending to the whole process yourself, procure your supply of bulbs from a reliable seed store, or order by mail. The bulbs should be firm and plump. The easiest to grow and the most satisfactory are hyacinths, tulips, narcissus and freesia. They can be grown in pots, but success will be more certain with small boxes four to six inches deep and any size up to the regu-

A pan of forced crocuses. The big secret of success lies in securing a good root growth before a top growth starts

Few people realize that the gladiolus is an easily forced
bulb for indoor bloom. This variety is named Victory

lar " flat " (about 13x22 inches), according to the
number you wish in bloom at one time. All the
paraphernalia you will need is a supply of light,
rich soil (one-third old rotted manure, two-thirds
rotted turf-loam is good) a few fern or bulb pans,
boxes, and your bulbs. Begin operations early
in October. Cover the bottoms of your pots and
boxes, which should have ample drainage (see illustration) with an inch or so of coarse screenings,
charcoal lumps, pot fragments or sifted coal cinders
to assure good drainage. Cover this with an inch
or so of soil, and put the bulbs in place, setting them
firmly, right side up, and near enough almost to
touch each other. The " extra size " bulbs can go
a little further apart, but not more than two or three
inches. Then cover over and fill with the same soil,
until the bulbs are an inch or so below the surface
of the potting soil.

The Dutch or Cape Bulbs.—The next step is to
select your storage place, where the bulbs are to be
kept while making roots, and until they are wanted
to flower in the house. A dark, cold, dry cellar,
free from mice, will do. If this is not available use
the coldframe, if you have one, or simply dig a
trench, in any well drained spot, about one foot
deep, and long enough to hold your boxes and pots.
After placing them here give them a thorough
watering, and cover with six or eight inches of soil.
Cover freesias only two inches, with a light soil.

If you wish to keep tabs on your plantings, use a
long stake, with place for tag at the top, in each pan
or box.   Don't trust to your memory.

Your bulbs will need no further care until they
are ready to be brought in, except, on the approach
of freezing weather, to cover the trench with leaves,
or litter if they are kept outdoors.   In four or five
weeks bring in hyacinths and polyanthus narcissi.   Von Thol tulips may be had in bloom
by Christmas.   Success will be more certain with
the other tulips and large flowered narcissi if
you wait until the last of November before bringing them into the house.   Their growth outside will
have been almost entirely root growth; the first
leaves may have started, but will not be more than
an inch or two high.   Immediately upon bringing
them in, the bulbs should be given another good
watering, and from this time on should never be
allowed to suffer for water.   When the flower
spikes are half developed, a little liquid manure, or
nitrate of soda, or one of the prepared plant foods,
dissolved in water, will be of great benefit applied
about once a week.   The temperature for bulbs just
brought in should be at first only 45 to 50 degrees;
after a few days 10 degrees more.   In the ordinary
living-room a little ventilation by opened windows
will readily lower the temperature, but care should
be taken not to expose the growing plants to any
draft.   Forcing bulbs, like almost all other plants,

will be better and healthier with the maximum
amount of fresh air compatible with a sufficiently
high temperature.

The plants thus brought into water, light and
warmth, will grow with remarkable rapidity. Just
as the first buds are opening out is the ideal time to
use them as presents, as they will continue subjects
of daily attraction for a long time. Those that are
kept can be saved, either to plant out or use another
year. Let the soil gradually dry out when they
are through blooming, and when the tops are dead
take the bulbs from the soil, clean them and store
in a perfectly dry place, or in boxes, in dry sand.

The colors and other qualities of the many varieties of hyacinths, narcissi and tulips will be found
described in the fall catalogues of all the best seed-
houses.

As before stated, hyacinths, tulips, narcissi and
freesias are the most readily forced and the most
satisfactory bulbs. The beginner will do well, for
his first attempt, to confine himself to these. There
are, however, several more that respond to practically the same treatment, and whose various types
of beauty will repay handsomely the trouble of forcing them.

Ixias and *sparaxias* are two more of the Cape
group easily forced and well worth growing. They
like a cool temperature, 35 to 40 degrees at night,
even after having been brought in. They should

not be put in the dark or covered with earth after
potting, but started in a cool temperature, with
light.

Oxalis. Another very beautiful effect is had by
getting a hanging basket, or a pot-hanger with
which to suspend a six-inch or eight-inch bulb-pan,
and in it start some oxalis bulbs. They do not
need to be rooted first, but should be placed at once
in the light and heat (about 55 degrees). They
will send out spray after spray of beautiful flowers,
continuing in bloom for months. Dry off and rest
about June, if started in October; start again in the
fall. Freesias and oxalis, to be had in bloom by
Christmas, should be started in August.

Easter Lily (Lillium Harrisii) is universally
popular. It is usually bought from the florist in
bud or bloom, but may be grown in the house.
Large firm bulbs should be procured, and potted at
once in five or six inch pots, and given the same
treatment as above until root growth has been made,
when they will still be several months from flowering. When wanted for Easter they should be
brought into the house the first or second week in
November. Keep rather cool for two or three
weeks. Later they may be given a much higher
temperature. When the pots are covered with
roots, it is a good plan to carefully repot, setting
rather deep, so that the new roots starting above the
soil, may be of use.

Lillium candidum and *L. longiflorum* may be given the same treatment but will require a longer time in which to mature.

Calla (*Richardia Aethiopica*) The soil for callas should, where possible, be about one-third rotted cow manure. Otherwise make very rich soil with bone and whatever may be had but get the cow manure if possible. It also likes a great deal of water. Pot at once in large pots, give a thorough watering and keep cool and shaded for four or five weeks, until active growth begins. Then give more heat, keeping it about 60 degrees if you can. They will continue to bloom a long time. In the spring, after flowering ceases, dry off gradually and lay the pots on their sides in a shaded spot, and rest until August. Beside the large white calla most commonly seen, there are several other forms which will be found described in good catalogues, among them Tom Thumb or Little Gem, a dwarf sort; *Elliottiana*, the Yellow calla; Godfrey, a dwarf ever-blooming sort, especially desirable as a pot plant where, as is often the case, the ordinary large white sort is too big to be managed conveniently; *albomaculata,* white with purple throat, etc. The red and black callas are arums.

Cyclamen. While these beautiful flowers may be grown from seed it is much easier for the amateur to get the bulbs or a growing plant. If the former, pot in four- or five-inch pots, using a light compost and giving little water at first.   Repot as needed.   Shade during summer and syringe frequently, give 55 to 60 degrees in winter, with liquid manure while flowering.   When the leaves begin to look yellowish, dry off, and give a short rest but don't let them get dry enough to shrivel.

The Gloxinia (Sinningia speciosa) may receive much the same treatment but is a summer bloomer. The bulbs or dried roots should be potted up in February or March and kept growing on and repotted.   One of their valuable characteristics is the great range of colors and combinations in the flowers, which are freely produced.

The Amaryllis-like Group.   Amaryllis (*Hippeastrum*) is altogether too little known in its modern varieties.   Everyone has seen one of the old forms, red or red with a white stripe, with the lily-like flowers borne well aloft above scant foliage.   But the new named sorts are tremendous improvements and should by all means be tried, even if they seem expensive beside other bulbs, of which you can get a dozen for the price of one good amaryllis.   Remember, however, that the amaryllis is of the very easiest culture and will last for years.

Pot the bulbs up as soon as received — they come in November — and let them stay dormant awhile. In a month or two they will begin growth and flower (unfortunately) long before the leaves have made much of a show.   Do not dry off just because the flowers fade,— the plant has got to make its growth and store up food for next season. Continue to water and feed — outdoors in the summer — until the leaves begin to turn yellow; then dry off and store in a cool place until the bulbs again show signs of growth. The flowers are generally borne from January until May and come in shades of crimson, blood-red and white and attractive combinations of these colors.

Vallota purpurea is little known, but a very useful plant for the window garden, resembling the amaryllis, but having evergreen foliage which, of course, gives it a distinct advantage. The flowers are reddish scarlet.

Imantophyllum miniatum is another very desirable evergreen foliaged bulb, having large amaryllislike flowers, red with a yellow throat. There are several varieties.

The African blue lily (*Agapanthus umbellatus*) is quite like the above but the flowers are bright blue, a large number forming each umbel, so that it is one of the most striking of plants. It naturally flowers in the summer (being carried through the winter by storing in the cellar), but by changing the resting season may be flowered in the spring. Unlike most of the other bulbs in this group, they should be repotted in rich soil every year, to do their best. Beside the above there are varieties with white and with double flowers and one with variegated leaves. They form a most interesting group.

The Blood Flower *(Hœmanthus)* has very beautiful flowers but they are produced in advance of the foliage. Give the same treatment as amaryllis.

The above group will make a very unusual and desirable collection, easily managed, and giving satisfaction for a good many years.

Tuberous Begonia. While this is not a bulb, strictly speaking, it is treated in about the same way as the bulbs. The tubers should be started in pots and not much larger than themselves, in a light, rich soil, using old cow manure and leaf-mould, if available, to secure these characteristics. Repot as often as necessary until seven- or eight-inch pots are filled. Then feed while blooming. The tubers are dried off after growth, taken from the pots and stored in sand or sawdust to prevent shriveling. They are among the most satisfactory of flowers, but as their development has taken place largely within the last ten years or so, they are not yet nearly so widely known as they deserve. For flowering either in pots or outdoors they rank among the very best. Avoid direct sunlight.

Gladiolus. This magnificent flower has gained rapidly during recent years, but few flower-lovers seem to realize as yet that it may be easily forced indoors. Pot up the bulbs in December,

using a rich soil and setting them just even with it
and covering with half an inch of gritty sand.
America, May and Shakespeare are three of the
best varieties for forcing but new ones are being
produced every year. Keep cool until a good root
growth is made, then shift to four- or five-inch pots
and keep in a room of 45 to 50 degrees at night.

Caladiums. While the fancy-leaved caladiums
require a higher temperature than most house plants,
they will repay the extra care and heat demanded
in cases where it can be given. Start in February.
Cover under and over with fine sphagnum moss,
kept moist, and give 60 degrees until the roots start,
which they will do quickly. Then pot in rather
small pots, using a rich, light soil, with plenty of
leaf-mould and sand. Water sparingly at first;
shift on and give manure water as the leaves develop. Give all the light possible without letting
the direct sunlight strike them during the heat of
the day. Fifty-five degrees at night is the minimum
temperature to allow. When the leaves begin to die
dry off and treat as for begonias.

Lily-of-the-Valley (Convallaria majalis) may be
forced in the house where sufficient bottom heat
can be given and they are very desirable flowers,
possessing a grace, beauty and fragrance seldom
combined. Get " cold storage pips " and place in
deep flats of pure sand. They may be stored in the
cold and brought in as desired. Increase the

temperature gradually until by placing over a radiator or in some other exceptionally warm place, 75 to 80 degrees is given at the bottom of the box. Keep covered from the light until the buds show when the shading should be gradually removed.

Iris. The Spanish iris makes a very desirable plant for forcing and the plants are easily managed. A list of colors, etc., will be found in most of the fall bulb catalogues. They are quite distinct from the Japanese and German irises ordinarily seen outdoors. Start same as caladium, but they do not require so much heat.

Spirea (Astilbe Japonica). Several varieties of this beautiful flower are good for forcing. When the roots are received pot up in light, rich soil, water thoroughly, and set in a shaded place. Remove to the cellar or a deep coldframe as freezing weather comes on. Do not let the soil dry out. After the first of January bring into heat gradually. Sprinkle frequently as growth develops.

Ranunculus or buttercups, listed in the catalogues as Turkish, Persian and French, are very easily grown flowers. They have fleshy roots which are given the same treatment as Cape bulbs, i.e., started in light.

Poppy-flowered Anemones (A. fulgens and *A. coronaria)* are also easily grown in the same way. They come in a variety of colors, including reds, whites, and blues. They are very cheery little flowers, two inches or so across, and well worth giving a few pots to.

Several of the bulbs are easily grown in water, or pebbles and water, with no soil at all. The best known of these is the Chinese Sacred Lily. The Golden Chinese Lily is not so well known but very desirable. Hyacinths are easily grown in pure water; a special vase called the " hyacinth glass " being made for the purpose.

CHAPTER XVI

MANY of the plants ordinarily set outdoors in pots, or planted in the flower beds, could be much more effectively used in veranda boxes, window-boxes, vases or hanging baskets.

The veranda boxes are generally about eight by six inches, made as described on page 9, and of the right length to fit some window-sill, or the corner or top of a veranda railing.

Arrangements for watering should be made as convenient as possible, as this work is almost sure to be more or less neglected during the hot months when it needs frequent and thorough attention.

The soil used should be porous and very rich, as many plants will have to get their nourishment from a very limited space.

The majority of the plants described in the foregoing pages may be utilized successfully in box work; which ones in any particular case should depend on circumstances, such for instance as whether the boxes will be in partial shade, or strong sunlight; or whether in a sheltered or a wind-

Iceland poppies are not often seen in the window-box, as it takes many blooms to make a good showing

Window-boxes are at their best when containing only one or two kinds of bloom, part of it hanging down

It is not necessary to have your window garden consist of tomato cans or old saucers—a little ingenuity will suggest such improvements as this movable plant table

swept position. A favorite combination is dracae-
nas, Nutt or Beauté Poitevine, with the variegated
vinca as a front border. The lover of plants de-
sirous of artistic effects will not be content, however,
to go by fixed rules where so many opportunities for
expression of individual taste are offered.

There are two warnings to be given in addition
to the suggestions above. Do not attempt to crowd
too many plants into the small space available; remember that as a safe rule the most pleasing results will be obtained by the use of a very few kinds
and colors. A good way to be sure of not making
mistakes is to fill the boxes to within three or four
inches of the top, arrange the plants, still in their
pots, until a satisfactory picture is designed, and
then fill up with soil and plant.

Vases usually have three serious drawbacks; they
are very restricted in size, are exposed to the most
drying action of winds and sun, and are not conveniently watered. The last two disadvantages can
be to some extent overcome by placing them in situ-
ations at least partially sheltered and shaded, and
by running a half-inch or three-quarter inch pipe
(which may be bought second hand for two
to four cents a foot, while good hose costs sixteen
to eighteen), a few inches under the sod and up to
the top of the vase. Such a pipe should be detached
and drained in the fall and will last many years; the
few feet running up to the vase will be sufficiently

concealed by the vines and reasonably inconspicuous.

Where such precautions are not taken, restrict the plants used to those doing well in the heat, and a dry soil; one of the best is the ice plant (*Mesembryanthemum*) with flowers of pink or white, very freely produced.

There is no prettier way of displaying plants than in the hanging basket, either in the house or on the porch. That one so seldom sees them is undoubtedly due to the fact that few people seem to know how to fill and take care of them. In the first place, the basket should be as large as possible — a size or so larger than you think you ought to have, for what reason you will see in the following.

Get a supply of sphagnum moss, and line the entire inner surface, sides as well as bottom, an inch in thickness; press down compactly, then fill nearly full of light, rich prepared soil, and put in the plants; something tall and graceful in the center, compact and dwarf-growing around this, and vines around the edges. Astonishingly beautiful results may be had with small baskets by using only one sort of plant in each, such as oxalis, ivy geranium or some trailing flowering vines. Cover the surface of the soil between the plants with clean live sphagnum moss. This will both add to the appearance and conserve the moisture.

The best way by far to water hanging baskets is to have them so arranged that they may be taken down easily and allowed to soak until thoroughly wet in a tub or pail of water — which will take some time, as the moss will be like a dry sponge. Let them drain until dripping ceases and hang in place again.

If the above method is adhered to, you are sure to meet with success that will prove most gratifying.

CHAPTER XVII

I F the suggestions for taking proper care of
plants, detailed in a former chapter, are carefully followed, and they are given plenty of
fresh air and not crowded together, insects should
not cause serious trouble.

No matter how careful one may be, however,
they are almost certain to put in an appearance
and steps to combat them must be taken immediately. Remember, however, that the best remedy
is prevention, and the best prevention is to have
good strong healthy plants.

The two troubles perhaps the most common are
neither insects nor disease. They are gas and sour
soil.

The faintest trace of furnace gas or of illuminat-
ing gas will cause trouble, indicated by the yellow-
ing and falling of the leaves and unsatisfactory
development of buds. Where there is no way of
eliminating the presence of these gases the only way
to success with the plants — unless they can be entirely shut off in an enclosed place as suggested in
Chapter II — is to take every possible care about
leaks, and to give all the fresh air possible.

Sour soil is the result of improper drainage con-

ditions, too much water, or both. It causes the
leaves to turn yellow and checks new growth.
Making right the harmful conditions will usually
renew the health of the plant, but in bad cases it will
be far better to remove the earth, wash the soil from
the roots, carefully clean the pot — if the same one
is to be used — and repot in good porous fresh
earth. Keep on the dry side until growth is re-
sumed.

As a rule, insects do much more damage to house
plants than is caused by diseases. One characteristic of nearly all plant insects which will astonish
the amateur is the marvelous rapidity with which
they increase. One to-day, and to-morrow a mil-
lion, seems no exaggeration. While it may be true
that, as one of our erstwhile best-selling heroes
said, "a few fleas is a good thing for a dog; they
keep him from broodin' on bein' a dog," a few bugs
are certainly not good for a plant, because in a day
or two there will be enough of them to endanger its
life and surely, quickly to ruin its appearance.
Never let the bugs get a start. If you take them in
time they're easy: if not you have a very difficult
and disagreeable task on your hands.

PLANT ENEMIES

Aphis. Aphis or green plant louse is the most
commonly encountered of all the insect pests. It
used to be dreaded, but with modern methods

it may be readily and effectively exterminated.
There are several forms and colors of these pests.
If you have attempted plant-growing you are undoubtedly familiar with them. In the house, shaded
places, crowded plants, poor ventilation, dry plants,
all furnish environment favorable to the development of aphids. Change these conditions at once.
The old method of fighting used to be by burning
moistened tobacco stems, or steeping them in water
and making a very weak tea for spraying. But
either was a difficult, disagreeable and unsatisfactory method. There are now on the market three
forms of tobacco all of which are easy to use and
efficient. Tobacco dust — but it must be strong
and made especially for the purpose; liquid nicotine,
to be diluted and sprayed on according to directions;
and prepared paper for fumigating. The last is perhaps the most effective. Besides these, and in my experience pleasanter and quicker, is the comparatively
new compound called Aphine, which can be had
from almost any seedsman in quart tins — enough
to make five gallons of very effective spray, which
will not discolor flowers or foliage.

Red Spider. This very serious pest is about the
size and color of a grain of red pepper —although
sometimes appearing brown or dull red. To make
himself inconspicuous, he works on the under side
of the leaves and behind a tiny web, but his presence is soon made manifest by the leaves upon which

he is at work, which first turn light green, then
show minute yellow spots, turn yellow and finally
drop off.

The red spider is very tenacious of life, and hard
to get rid of when he is allowed time to become
well established. The best weapon to use against
him, where it can be done, is clear cold water with
as much force as possible against the under side of
the foliage.   Damp atmosphere assists in the work;
so keep the air damp, and be on a sharp lookout.
Evaporated sulphur, or flowers of sulphur dusted
upon the leaves will also help.

Where the collection of plants is not too large a
one, the quickest and most certain way to be rid of
the spider is to dip the top of each plant quickly two
or three times into hot water — 140 to 165 degrees.
Although uncomfortable to the hand, water of this
temperature will not injure the tenderest plant.   It
is effective against aphis and mealy bug, as well as
against the spider.

Mealy Bug.   The mealy bug inhabits a white,
cottony looking mass, which is easily seen.   Remove this covering and the real intruder is there.
It is most fond of the soft-wooded plants, such as
coleus and fuchsias, thrives in a hot, dry atmosphere,
and will keep out of sight, if not watched for, in a
mass of leaves or under some branch axis, until
there are a large number.

If they are discovered before multiplying to any

great extent, exterminate them with a fine brush
or feather dipped in alcohol, coal-oil or kerosene,
any of which, if applied directly to them, will kill
them on the spot.

Scale. The scales infesting house plants are of
two kinds. The more common is the brown scale,
which has a hard, slightly convex, circular shell, one-
quarter of an inch or so in diameter. The white
scale is much smaller, and soon forms quite dense
colonies. Both attack the thick-leaved, smooth-
barked plants, such as palms, ferns, lemons, and
abutilons. They do not appear to be doing any
damage, but invisibly suck the juices of the plant.
They should be destroyed at once. This is accomplished by the use of fir-tree-oil soap, whale-oil soap,
or kerosene emulsion and a stiff brush.

Thrips. These do not often appear in the house,
but may where plants are crowded in a shady place.
They eat the substance of the leaves, leaving only
the skeleton structure. They are small, about a
quarter of an inch long, and brown or black.
Aphine, kerosene emulsion or Paris green (one
teaspoonful to twelve quarts of water) will keep
them quiet.

Root Aphis. Sometimes the leaves of a healthy
plant will begin to look sickly with no apparent
cause. It may be found upon examination that the
blue root aphis is at work, clinging in clusters to
the rootlets. Remove and wash away the soil, and

then wash the roots in whale-oil soap suds, and re-pot in fresh soil. If no fresh soil is available, to-bacco tea or tobacco dust should be washed into the soil every other day for a week.

Soil Worms. The common earthworms some-times find their way into a pot, and while they do not seem to bother the roots, I should judge from ob-servation that they render the soil next to useless, especially in small pots. Another worm, or rather larva, sometimes to be found, is very small and hatches into a small white fly. If numerous, they do a good deal of damage. The treatment recom-mended for root aphis will get rid of them; or lime water (slake a piece of fresh lime the size of an apple in a pail of water, drawing off the water after settling), if used freely will kill them.

DISEASES

There are but two plant diseases likely to attack plants in the house: fungus and mildew. The first seems to be a sort of decomposition of the leaf, leav-ing a black, powdery residue. It is combated by spraying with bordeaux. Bordeaux can now be had in paste or powder form, which for small quantities is much better than to try to mix it yourself.

Mildew causes the tenderest leaves to curl up and some of them seem to be covered with a white powder. Flowers of sulphur, dusted over the plants while the foliage is damp, is the standard remedy.

For the sake of ready reference, the foregoing is

condensed in the following simple table of plant
insects and diseases.

INSECT OR DISEASE	CONDITIONS SUPPORTING GROWTH	REMEDIES
Aphis, green and black	Shade; poor ventilation; thick foliage	Aphine; tobacco-dust or tea; kerosene emulsion; hot water bath; insect powder.
Aphis, blue.......	Stunted growth; lack of water...	Whale-oil soap solution; re-potting; tobacco tea applied to roots.
Thrips, ¼ inch, long, brown or black; they eat.	Shaded places; crowded plants..	Kerosene emulsion; Paris green—1 teaspoon to 12 quarts water.
Mealy bugs } Other scale insects ....}	Corners; close, dry air	Brush off; coal-oil; kerosene emulsion; hot water.
Red spider........	Hot, dry atmosphere	Moisture, sulphur, hot water.
Rose-beetle		Hand picking; wood ashes.
White flies (Aleyrodes)	Dry foliage.......	Kerosene emulsion.
Slugs	Dark corners; dampness; decaying wood....	Air-slaked lime, sweetened bran and Paris green.
Ants		Insect powder; molasses traps.
Angleworms	Dampness; heavy soil	Lime; lime-water; tobacco tea, and tobacco dust washed into soil.
White grub.......	Manure not old enough Destroy.	
Fungous leaf spot	Shocks; checks...	Bordeaux; Fungine.
Mildew	Checks	Flowers of sulphur; Fungine.

To make the kerosene emulsion, use 2 ounces of soap (whale-oil is much better than the common), 1 quart of boiling water (over brisk fire), 2 quarts of kerosene oil.   Dissolve the soap in boiling water, remove from fire, and add oil.   Churn or beat until of the consistency of cream.   If correctly mixed, the emulsion, on cooling, will adhere without oiliness to glass.   Use rain water, if possible; if not, add a little baking soda to the water.

For scale insects, dilute with 10 parts of water; for aphis and soft insects, with 15 or 20 parts water.   In using kerosene emulsion, apply in fine spray.   Remember it must come in contact with the insect to be effective.

CHAPTER XVIII

THE following list of implements and materials is suggestive rather than imperative. While all these things are useful many successful flower growers get along without many of them. At the same time, if one adds to the garden outfit from time to time, the expense will hardly be noticed and in the course of two or three years a fairly complete set will be accumulated. Do not feel in the least that in the meantime you cannot grow flowers successfully.

FOR MIXING SOIL

Spade. A good long-bladed sharp instrument should be procured, for use both in taking up plants and in cutting out sod, etc., for the compost heap and in " cutting down " the same for repiling.

Hoe. Get a long blade with a straight edge. See that the ferrule and shank are of one piece if you do not want to be bothered with a loose head.

Sieve. For small amounts of soil, an ordinary round coal ash sieve is just the thing. It is a good thing to have as it will insure getting soil for seeds and small pots to the proper degree of fineness.

Trowel. Don't buy a cheap trowel. They may be had for fifteen or twenty cents but a fifty-cent one will outlast a dozen of these and not break just when you need it most.

SOIL INGREDIENTS

A sufficient quantity of soil constitutents should be kept on hand in barrels or covered boxes. Store where they will not dry out.

Rich Loam or Rotted Sod. This is the basis of most plant soils. Keep a good supply ahead, that it may be thoroughly decomposed.

Sand. What is known as "Builders' Sand," medium, coarse and gritty, is the proper kind. Contrary to some horticultural superstitions, it makes no difference what the color is, "silver" or gray, red, white or yellow.

Leaf-mould. Easily procured by scraping aside the top layer near some stone wall or hollow in the woods where leaves collect and rot from year to year.

Sphagnum moss is another very valuable accessory. It can be gathered in most swampy places or bought cheaply at the florist's.

Peat. Not obtainable in all localities, but it can be bought cheap from florists. Found under mucky bog-swamps but must be thoroughly dried and pulverized before use.

Bone meal. This is invaluable for enriching plant

soil. (See page 19.) The fine sort, sometimes called bone flour, is the quickest acting. For plants that stay potted for several years, it is best to use about two-thirds of the coarse-ground.

FOR PLANTING AND TRANSPLANTING

Transplanting fork. This can be had in malleable iron for fifteen cents and as it is not submitted to hard strains, like a trowel, will do as well as the seventy-five-cent imported sorts. It will save the life of innumerable seedlings, in lifting them from the seed box.

Dibber. You can make two or three of various sizes in a few minutes from a piece of soft pine. They are used for pricking off and repotting. It will often be convenient to have one end bluntly pointed and the other rather flat.

Sub-irrigation tray. The use of this convenient method of watering is described on page 24 and illustrated facing page 28. The tinsmith will make you a tray for fifty or seventy-five cents. It will certainly pay to have one if you attempt to grow many fine-seeded flowers.

Watering can. As this accessory is more used perhaps than any other, and as the quality of the work it does is very important, it is poor economy to buy a cheap one. The Wotherspoon type, sold by most seed houses, is the best. It has brass fittings which will not rust, tighten or rot out and a coarse and a fine brass nozzle with each pot. They cost from two to three dollars, according to size, but are well worth the money.

Pots. A good smooth red pot adds not a little to the looks of a plant. For the ordinary collection of house plants three shapes, quite distinct, are desirable : " Standard " the sort ordinarily seen; " Pans," very shallow for their width and used for bulbs, or ferns (facing p. 116) ; and " Rose " pots, or those exceptionally deep. The latter are good for plants requiring large root room, such as single bulbs, or plants demanding exceptionally thorough drainage.

Bulb glasses. These are constructed especially to support the bulb, while permitting the roots to grow down into the water. They come in different shapes and colors and are not expensive.

Hanging baskets. Attractive baskets can now be had cheaply. They are made of wire, rustic work or earthenware, and no plant lover should be without one or two, as they offer a most effective way of displaying plants. Use picture wire to support them, as cord is apt to rot and break. They should be hung so as to be easily taken down.

Boxes. While these may be home-made, as described on page 9, it is often desirable to purchase one of the ornamental sorts now on the market. Many of them are hideous, but there are artistically designed ones. The " self-watering " box is a great labor-saver and well worth getting where one can afford the investment, as they will last for years.

In addition to the above there are a number of other devices often convenient to use.

Brackets, frequently make possible the accommodation of a number of extra plants and show them off to the best advantage, especially vines and drooping plants. They are readily secured by screws to the window casing.

Pot-hangers, can be had for a few cents each and used to convert pots of any size into " Hanging baskets." They very often solve the problem of what to do with a choice plant that is beginning to take up too much room.

Pot-covers, made of water-proof material are now to be had in a great assortment of styles and colors and are very useful, especially in connection with potted plants used as gifts.

Plant-stakes. Often any old stake is used for supporting drooping plants, such as fuchsias. A much better one can easily be made by taking a round stick, say one-half or three-fourths of an inch in diameter and boring small holes through it with a gimlet. Stout pieces of wire, of a size that will fit snugly are inserted and twisted once around to reinforce the wood. These may then be bent readily to any angle and thus made to conform with needs

of the particular plant being supported. If one
has a soldering outfit, the main stake may be made
of heavy wire.

Raffia. This may be bought cheaply at the florist's and is much better than twine for tying up
plants and similar purposes, as it is soft and broad
— a dried, ribbon-like grass. It may be had stained
green and with green stakes makes the support of a
plant practically invisible.

Syringe. If only a few plants are kept, a rubber
bulb plant sprinkler may do for syringing them.
But if one wants to combat insects and keep plants
healthy with the least trouble, a small florist's brass
syringe will prove a good investment. With ordinary care they will last a lifetime. It will also be
useful for applying insecticides in liquid form.

Fertilizers. In addition to the chemicals, etc.,
described in Chapter III, there are to be had concentrated plant foods in tablet form. These are
very convenient to use, and a box kept on hand will
frequently prove useful. If any number of plants
are kept, however, an old metal pail and a small dip-
per, for mixing and applying liquid manure, should
have a place in the tool outfit and be used frequently. Never apply liquid manure when the soil
is dry.

Part Two—Home Glass

CHAPTER XIX

ITS OPPORTUNITIES

IT cannot be said that America has yet reached the gardening age. There is no doubt, however, that the appreciation of flowers, and the liking for things horticultural in general, is growing rapidly. The stimulus that compels hundreds to turn with delight to the joy in the creative work of growing things arises from a sound foundation. Comparatively few people, however, realize that this pleasure can be had by them around the entire circle of the months. They look forward to planting time in the spring and accept as inevitable the cessation of their gardening adventures with the first frost.

It is to such people that the message of home glass must come as good tidings indeed. For them the gentle art of gardening under glass has seemed a distant and mysterious thing. Little indeed have they realized how easily it might be brought within reach; that instead of being an expensive luxury it would be by no means impossible to make it a paying investment, yielding not only pleasure but profit as well.

As a matter of fact, when one's mind is once made up not to sacrifice the pleasures of gardening for six months every year, a little energy, ingenuity and a very few dollars will go a long way in providing the necessary equipment.

Nor is the care of the ordinary flowers, and the vegetables suited for winter use, such a complicated profession that the beginner cannot achieve quite a considerable measure of success with his or her very first attempts, provided that regular care is given the work in hand. It is a much easier task than succeeding with plants in the house, notwithstanding the fact that general opinion is to the contrary.

It is not necessary to start in on a large scale. A very few square feet of soil, where all the conditions can be controlled as they are under glass, will produce an amazing amount. Take for instance lettuce grown for the home table. How good it is right fresh and crisp from the soil compared to the wilted or artificially revived bunches one can get at the grocer's! Outdoors you put it a foot apart in rows a foot and a half apart; a patch 3 x 10 feet would give you twenty heads. In the home garden under glass you set out a batch of Grand Rapids lettuce plants, one of the very best in quality, six inches each way, so that a little piece of bench 3 x 10 feet would give you one hundred heads (which incidentally at the grocer's would cost you $10. or $12.—enough good money to buy glass for a quite roomy little lean-to).   (See page 164.)

Details of construction, etc., are given in the following pages, but the most important thing of all is
just to make up your mind that you will have a little greenhouse of your own.   If you once decide to
have it the way can be found, for the necessary cash
outlay is very small indeed.

Think of the variety of ways you could use such
a winter garden!   Not only may lettuce, radishes,
tomatoes, cucumbers, beets and other vegetables be
had out of season, but you can get a better start
with your garden than ever before — put it weeks
and weeks ahead of the old sow-out-in-the-ground
way.   And then consider the flowers!   A dozen
carnation plants, for instance, would occupy about
six square feet of room, say 2 x 3 feet of bench, and
would supply you comfortably with blossoms all
winter long — nice fresh ones outlasting twice over
the cold storage blooms from the retail florist's —
to say nothing of the added value of having them
actually home grown.

It is surprising how most people over-estimate the difficulties
and expense of maintaining a small greenhouse. In relation
to the pleasure one brings, the cost is exceedingly small

A lean-to type of greenhouse, such as has been built on the east wall of this house, is within reach of almost any owner of a small country place

CHAPTER XX

THE simplest form of home glass is the cold-frame. The simplest hothouse is the manure heated coldframe or hotbed.

The following directions for making the frames and preparing the soil for them are taken from the author's *Home Vegetable Gardening*.

For the ordinary garden, all the plants needed may be started successfully in hotbeds and cold-frames. The person who has had no experience with these has usually an exaggerated idea of their cost and of the skill required to manage them. The skill is not as much a matter of expert knowledge as of careful regular care, daily. Only a few minutes a day, but every day. The cost need be but little, especially if one is a bit handy with tools. The sash which serves for the cover, and is removable, is the important part of the structure. Sash may be had, ready glazed and painted, at from $2.50 to $3.50 each, and with care they will last ten or even twenty years, so you can see at once that not a very big increase in the yield of your garden will be required to pay interest on the investment. Or you can buy the sash unglazed, at

a proportionately lower price, and put the glass in
yourself, if you prefer to spend a little more time
and less money. However, if you are not familiar
with the work, and want only a few sash, I would
advise purchasing the finished article. In size they
are three feet by six.

Frames upon which to put the sash covering may
also be bought complete, but here there is a chance
to save money by constructing your own frames —
the materials required being 2 x 4 inch lumber for
posts, and inch-boards; or better, if you can easily
procure them, plank 2 x 12 inches.

So far as these materials go the hotbed and coldframe are alike. The difference is that while the
coldframe depends for its warmth upon catching
and holding the heat of the sun's rays, the hotbed
is artificially heated by fermenting manure, or in
rare instances, by hot water or steam pipes.

In constructing the hotbed there are two methods
used; either placing the frames on top of the manure heap or by putting the manure within the
frames. The first method has the advantage of
permitting the hotbed to be made upon frozen
ground, when required in the spring. The latter,
which is the better, must be built before the ground
freezes, but is more economical of manure. The
manure in either case should be that of grain-fed
horses, and if a small amount of straw bedding, or
leaves — not more, however, than one-third of the

latter — be mixed among it, so much the better.
Get this manure several days ahead of the time
wanted for use and prepare by stacking in a compact, tramped down heap. Turn it over after three
or four days, and re-stack, being careful to put the
manure from the top and sides of the pile now on
the inside.

Having now ready the heating apparatus and the
superstructure of our miniature greenhouse, the
building of it is a very simple matter. If the
ground is frozen, spread the manure in a low, flat
heap nine or ten feet on each side, a foot and a half
deep, and as long as the number of sash to be used
demands. A cord of manure thus furnishes a bed
for about three sash, not counting for the ends of
the string or row. This heap should be well trodden down and upon it should be placed the box or
frame upon which the sash are to rest. In using
this method it will be more convenient to have the
frame made up beforehand and ready to place upon
the manure, as shown in one of the illustrations.
This should be at least twelve inches high at the
front and some half a foot higher at the back. Fill
in with at least four inches — better six — of good
garden soil containing plenty of humus so that it
may allow water to soak through readily.

The other method is to construct the frames on
the ground before severe freezing, and in this case
the front should be at least twenty-four inches high,

part of which — not more than half — may be below the ground level. The 2 x 12 inch planks, when used, are handled as follows: stakes are driven in to support the back plank some two or three inches above the ground,— which should, of course, be level. The front plank is sunk two or three inches into the ground and held upright by stakes on the outside, nailed on. Remove enough dirt from inside the frame to bank up the planks about halfway on the outside. When this banking has frozen to a depth of two or three inches, cover with rough manure or litter to keep frost from striking through. The manure for heating should be prepared as above and put in to the depth of a foot, trodden down, first removing four to six inches of soil to be put back on top of the manure,—a cord of the latter, in this case, serving seven sashes. The vegetables to be grown, and the season and climate, will determine the depth of manure required — it will be from one to two feet,— the latter depth seldom being necessary.

It must not be overlooked that this manure, when spent for heating purposes, is still as good as ever to enrich the garden, so that the expense of putting it in and removing it from the frames is all that you can fairly charge up against your experiment with hotbeds, if you are interested to know whether they really pay.

The exposure for the hotbeds should be where

the sun will strike most directly and where they
will be sheltered from the north.   Put up a fence
of rough boards, five or six feet high, or place the
frames south of some building.

The coldframe is constructed practically as in the
hotbed, except that if manure is used at all it is for
the purpose of enriching the soil where lettuce, radishes, cucumbers or other crops are to be grown
to maturity in it.

All this may seem like a lot of trouble to go for
such a small thing as a packet of seed.   In reality it
is not nearly so much trouble as it sounds, and then,
too, this is for the first season only.   You will have
a well built frame lasting for years — forever, if
you want to take a little more time and make it of
concrete instead of boards.

But now that the frame is made, how to use it is
the next question.

The first consideration must be the soil.   It
should be rich, light, friable.   There are some garden loams that will do well just as taken up, but as
a rule better results will be obtained where the soil
is made up specially, as follows : rotted sods two
parts, old rotted manure one part, and enough coarse
sand added to make the mixture fine and crumbly,
so that, even when moist, it will fall apart when
pressed into a ball in the hand.   Such soil is best
prepared by cutting out sod, in the summer, where
the grass is green and thick, indicating a rich soil.

Along old fences or the roadside where the wash has settled will be good places to get limited quantities. These should be cut with considerable soil and stacked, grassy sides together, in layers in a compost pile. If the season proves very dry, occasionally soak the heap through. In late fall put in the cellar, or wherever solid freezing will not take place, enough to serve for spring work under glass. The amount can readily be calculated; soil for three sash, four inches deep, for instance, would take eighteen feet or a pile three feet square and two feet high. The fine manure (and sand, if necessary) may be added in the fall or when using in the spring. Here again it may seem to the amateur that unnecessary pains are being taken. I can but repeat what has been suggested all through these pages, that it will require but little more work to do the thing the best way as long as one is doing it at all, and the results will be not only better, but practically certain — and that is a tremendously important point about all gardening operations.

While the coldframe and hotbed offer great advantages — especially in the way of room — over growing plants and starting seed in the house, they are nevertheless incomparably less useful than the simplest small greenhouse. Plants may be wintered over in them, violets may be grown in them, lettuce may be grown late in the fall and early in the spring, and followed by cucumbers. But they are not convenient to work in.   One is dependent on the weather.   They are not satisfactorily under control.   Take, for instance, one of those dark fall days, with a cold nasty drizzle cutting down on a slant, or one of those bright sunny and cloudy chill-winded spring days, when no pleasure is to be had out-of-doors.   Under the shelter of your little glass roof, where you can make your own weather, what fun it is to be potting up a batch of cuttings, or putting in a few packets of choice seed for the extra early garden!   There is nothing like it.

CHAPTER XXI

THE CONSTRUCTION OF CONSERVATORIES AND SMALL GREENHOUSES

HAVE you ever stepped from the chill and dreariness of a windy day, when it seems as if the very life of all things growing were shrunk to absolute desolation, into the welcome warmth and light and fragrance, the beauty and joy of a glass house full of green and blossoming plants? No matter how small it was, even though you had to stoop to enter the door, and mind your elbows as you went along, what a good, glad comfortable feeling flooded in to you with the captive sunlight! What a world of difference was made by that sheet of glass between you and the outer bitterness and blankness. Doubtless such an experience has been yours. Doubtless, too, you wished vaguely that you could have some such little corner to escape to, a stronghold to fly to when old winter lays waste the countryside. But April came with birds, and May with flowers, and months before the first dark, shivery days of the following autumn, you had forgotten that another winter would come on, with weeks of cheerless, uncomfortable weather. Or possibly you did not forget, until you had investigated the matter of greenhouse building and found that even a very small house, built to order, was far beyond your means.

Do not misunderstand me as disparaging the construction companies: they do excellent work — and get excellent prices. You may not be able to afford an Italian garden, with hundreds of dollars' worth of rare plants, but that does not prevent your having a more modest garden spot, in which you have planned and worked yourself. Just so, though one of these beautiful glass structures may be beyond your purse, you may yet have one that will serve your purpose just as practically. The fact of the matter is, you can have a small house at a very small outlay, which will pay a good very good interest on your investment. With it you will be able to have flowers all the year round, set both your flower and vegetable garden weeks ahead in the spring, save many cherished plants from the garden, and have fresh green vegetables, such as lettuce, radishes, tomatoes and cucumbers that can readily be grown under glass. And you will be surprised, if you can give the work some personal attention, or, better still, have the fun of doing a little of the actual building yourself, at how small an outlay you can put up a substantial structure of practical size, say 20 feet by 10 — of the " lean-to " form.

By way of illustration let us see what the ma-

terial for such a house would cost, and how to erect
it. Almost every dwelling house has some sheltered corner or wall where some glass "lean-to"
could easily be added, and the shape and dimensions
can be made to suit the special advantages offered.
We will consider a simple house of the lean-to
type, requiring a wall, to begin with, 20 feet long

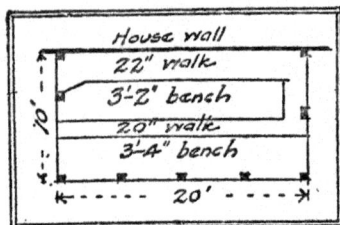

Fig. 2—Floor plan of the
lean-to type of green-
house shown in section
on the opposite page.

and 7 feet high, down to the ground, or a foot or
so below it, if you can dig out. Below is listed the
material such a house would require. With modern
patented framing methods such a house has been
estimated by greenhouse building companies to cost,
for the material only, from $325 to $400. Yet
you can have a wooden house that will serve your
purpose at a cost for materials of $61 and, if
you do not care to put it together yourself, a labor
cost of, say, one-third more.

As our north wall is already in place, we have
only four surfaces to consider, as the accompany-
ing diagram shows — namely, south wall, gable
ends, roof and openings. For the roof we will re-

quire a ridge against the wall of the dwelling house,
sash-bars running at right angles to this, a
" purlin," or support, midway of these, and a sill

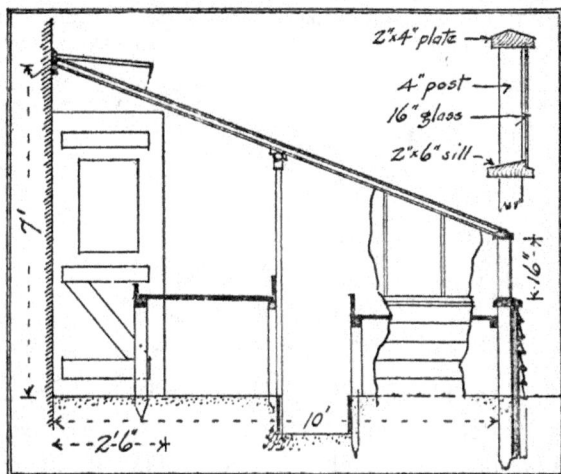

Fig. 3—A sectional view of a two-bench, 10 x 20 ft.
house built against the dwelling wall. If possible it
would be well to gain a steeper slope for the glass and
better headroom. The detail in the upper right hand
corner shows, at larger scale, the plate and front lights,
indicated just below in the main section.

for the lower ends. For the south wall we will
need posts, one row of glass, and boards and
" sheathing." For the gable ends, a board and
sheathing wall to the same height, and for the bal-
ance, sash-bars and glass. The required openings
will be a door or doors, and three ventilators, to give
a sufficient supply of fresh air.

For these the material required will be:

10 ft. of 2-in. x 4-in. ridge..............................	$ 0.80
13 10-ft. drip bars.......................................	3.25
2 10-ft. end bars..	1.00
5 6-ft. x 1¼-in. second-hand pipe posts.................	.50
20 ft. 1-in. second-hand iron pipe......................	1.00
4 1¼-in. x 1-in. clamps.................................	.50
20 ft. 2-in. x 4-in. eaves plate........................	1.60
20 ft. 2-in. x 6-in. sill...............................	2.20
15 1-in. pipe straps....................................	.50
18 ft. 2-in. x 4-in. sill, for gables...................	1.50
40 ft. side bars, random lengths, for gables............	1.00
3 ventilating sash for 3 24-in. x 16-in. lights.........	3.00
9 16-in. headers for ventilators........................	.40
6 hinges with screws for ventilators....................	.75
1 roll tar paper, single-ply............................	2.00
6 boxes 24-in. x 16-in. glass, B double thick...........	24.00
75 lbs. good greenhouse putty...........................	2.50
Total of items listed above...........................	$46.50

All of the above will have to come from a green-house material supply company, and prices given do not include freight charges. The following items may probably be bought more economically in your immediate vicinity, and the prices will vary in different sections of the country: —

Total of items listed above...........................	$46.50
240 ft. rough 1-in. boards.............................	7.50
6 posts, 4 in. thick, 6 ft. long, planed on one side........ }	
2 posts. 4 in. thick, 8 ft. long, planed on one side........	3.00
1000 shingles	4.00
Total cost of materials...............................	$61.00
Estimate of labor.....................................	20.00
Total cost of greenhouse..............................	$81.00

Level off a place about 22 x 12 feet, and set in

the posts as indicated in the plan on page 158, taking
care to get the lines for the ends of the house perfectly square with the wall, and exact in length.
This is best done by laying out your lines first with
stout string, and making your measurements ac-
curately on these. Then put in the posts for sides
and ends, setting these about three feet into the
ground, or, better still, in concrete. Put in the two
corner posts, which should be square first. Next
saw off all posts level at the proper height, and put
in place the 2 x 4 in. eaves plate on top of these and
the 2 x 6 in. sill just far enough below to take a 16 x
24 in. light of glass, with its upper edge snug in the
groove in lower side of plate, as shown in detail of
section on page 159. Fit the 2 x 6 in. sill about the
posts so that the mortice on same will just clear
the outside of posts. Then put on the siding on
sides and ends — first a layer of rough inch-boards,
running vertically, a layer, single or double, of tar
paper, and a second layer of boards, laid horizon-
tally, covering on the outside with shingles, clapboards or roofing paper. The five 7 ft. x 1 1-4 in.
pipe posts may now be placed loose in their holes,
and a walk dug out of sufficient depth to allow pas-
sage through the middle of the house. Rough
boards nailed to stakes driven into the ground, will
hold the earth sides of this in place.

Next, after having it sawed in two vertically
(thus making 20 ft), screw the ridge securely

to side of house at proper height, giving a thick coat of white lead at top to insure a tight joint with house. Now put one of the end bars in place, taking care to get it exactly at right angles with ridge, and then lay down the sash-bars, enough more than 16 in. apart to allow the glass to slip into place readily. Take a light of glass and try it between every fourth or fifth bar put into position, *at both ridge and eave,* as this is much easier than trying to remedy an error when half the glass is laid. Use " finishing " nails for securing the sash-bars, as they are easily split. Next, with chalk line mark the middle of the roof sash-bars, and secure to them the one-inch pipe purlin, which will then be ready to fasten to the uprights already in place. Next, make concrete by mixing two parts Portland cement, two of sand and four of gravel or crushed stone with sufficient water to make a mixture that will pour like thick mud, and put the iron pipe posts in their permanent positions, seeing that the purlin is level and the posts upright. (If necessary, the purlin can be weighted down until the concrete sets.) Then put into place the ventilators, glazed, and the headers for the same — short pieces of wood, cut to go in between the sash-bars,— and fit these up snugly against the lower edge of the ventilator sash.

When laying the glass in the roof, which will now be ready, use *plenty* of putty, worked sufficiently soft for the glass to be thoroughly bedded in it, and leaving no air-spaces or crevices for the rain to leak through later. If this work is carefully done, it will not be necessary to putty again on the outside of the glass, but it should be gone over with white lead and linseed oil. Be sure to place the *convex* surface of every light up. The panes should be lapped from 1-6 to 1-4 of an inch, and held securely in place with greenhouse glazing points, the double-pointed *bent* ones being generally used. The lights for the ends of the house may be " butted," that is, placed edge to edge, if you happen to strike good edges, but as a general thing, it will be more satisfactory to lap them a little. The woodwork, before being put together, should all receive a good priming coat of linseed oil in which a little ochre has been mixed, and a second coat after erection. I have suggested putting the glass in roof and sides before touching the benches, because this work can then be done under shelter in case bad weather is encountered. The benches can be arranged in any way that will be convenient, but should be about waist-high, and not over four or four and a half feet across, to insure easy handling of plants, watering, etc. Rough boards will do for their construction, and they should not be made so tight as to prevent the ready drainage of water. The doors may be bought, or made of boards covered with tar paper and shingles or roofing paper.

The house suggested above is used only by way

of illustration. It may be either too large or too
small for the purposes of some of the readers of this
book, and I shall therefore give very briefly descriptions of several other types of small houses,
some of which may be put up even more cheaply
than the above. The plainest is the sash lean-to
somewhat like Fig. 3, which is made by simply
securing to a suitable wall a ridge-piece to hold one
end of the sashes for the roof, and erecting a wall,
similar to the one described above, but without
glass, and with a plain, 2 x 4 in. piece for a sill, to
support the other ends. Either a single or double
row of sashes may be used, of the ordinary 3 x 6 foot
size. In the latter case, of course, a purlin and supporting posts, as shown in diagram, must be supplied. Every second or third top sash should be
hinged, to open for ventilation, and by tacking strips
over the edges of the sash where they come together, a very tight and roomy little house can be
put up quickly, easily and very cheaply. New
sash, glazed and painted one coat, can be bought
for $3 to $3.50 each. Ten of these would make a
very practical little house, fifteen feet long, and
over ten feet wide.

Another form of lean-to where there are windows is shown in another diagram. The even-
span house, of which type there are more erected
than of any other, is also shown. The cost of such
a house, say 21 feet wide, can be easily computed

Sash and frames for a coldframe or hotbed cost only about $3.00 per frame, 3 x 6 ft., and will serve to raise thousands of young plants for setting out in the spring

A simple and ingenious type of window greenhouse made from a single coldframe sash with side glazing and a shelf

An inside view of the same. Three shelves are available for plants in addition to the main shelf at the bottom

from the figures given in the first part of this chapter, the north wall, and purlin braces from the

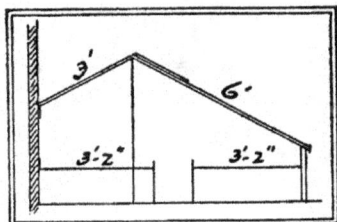

Fig. 4—A simple form
of lean-to greenhouse
where there is an avail-
able sheltering wall but
with first-story windows.
The inner slope or valley
should be drained

ridge posts, being the only details of construction
not included there.

A simple way of greatly increasing the capacity

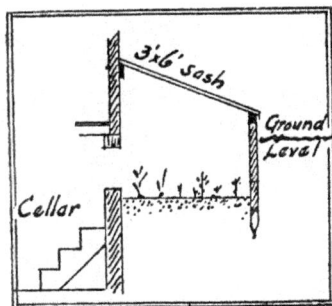

Fig. 5—The simplest of
all "greenhouses," which
is in reality little more
than a deep coldframe
with an opening into the
cellar

of the ordinary hotbed or coldframe, is to build it
next to a cellar window, so that it will receive some
artificial heat, and can be got at, from the inside, in
any weather. Several sashes can be used, and the

window extend to include as many of them as desired.

By all means get a little glass to use in connection with your garden this coming year. Put up

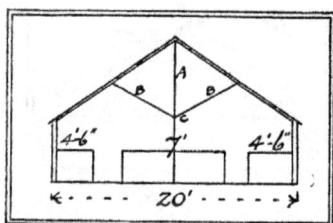

Fig. 6 — The regular even-span type. A indicates a row of pipe standards; BB, braces from these to the purlins. There is a fitting made for the junction C.

one of these small greenhouses, if you can: if not, get a few sash, at least. Don't put it off till next year; do it now!

In the next chapter we will take up the handling of vegetables and flowers in the small greenhouse. But don't be content to *read* about it. It's the pleasantest kind of *work* — try it yourself!

CHAPTER XXII

METHODS OF HEATING

IN the foregoing chapter on homemade greenhouses very brief reference was made to the
various methods of heating. It will be well
to understand a little more in detail how to heat
glass structures, as temperature is, next to moisture,
the most important factor of success. If steam or
hot water is used in the dwelling house and a greenhouse of the lean-to type is used, the problem becomes a very simple one, as additional pipes can be
run through the greenhouse. But as this advantage
is not always ready to hand, we will consider the
heating of an isolated house, and the principles in-
volved may be adapted to individual needs. There
are three systems of heating: flues (hot air), hot
water, and steam — the latter we need not take up
as it is economical only for larger structures than
the amateur is likely to have.

Heating by hot air carried through brick or tile
flues is the simplest and cheapest method for very
small houses. The best way of constructing such a
system is illustrated in the diagram adjoining, which
shows the flue returning into the chimney (after
traveling the length of the house and back). This

method does away with the greatest trouble with flue heating — a poor draft; for immediately the fire is started, the air in the chimney becomes heated,

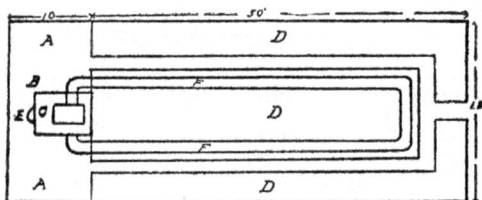

Fig. 7—The best arrangement for heating a greenhouse by hot air, is to run a brick or cement flue from the furnace around under the benches and into the chimney over the fire AA—storage space; B—furnace; C—chimney; DDD—benches; E—furnace door.

and rising, draws the hot air from the furnace around through the flue with a forced draft. This forced draft accomplishes three other good things: it does away with the escape of noxious gases into the greenhouses, lessens the accumulation of moisture and dust from wood smoke, and distributes the heat much more evenly throughout the house. The furnace may be built of solid brick, with doors and grates and an arched dome, and the flue should be of brick for at least one-third the length from the furnace into the house; for the rest of the way cement or vitrified drain pipe will be cheaper and better. The flue should have a gradual upward slope for its whole length and will vary in size with the

house to be heated, from five to eight or nine inches
in diameter, the latter being sufficient for a house
60 by 21 feet. The flue should be raised a little
from the ground, and at no point should any wood-

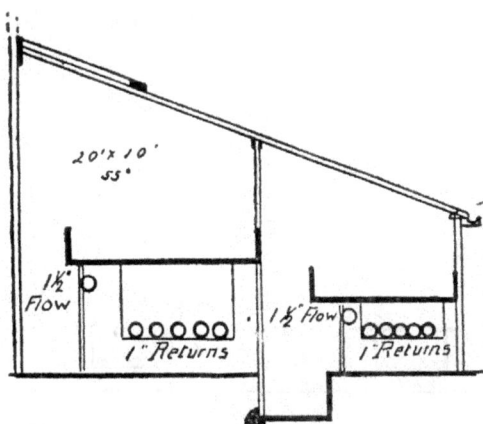

Fig. 8—Hot water is undoubtedly the most satisfactory method of heating the small greenhouse. The diagram shows a 1½-inch supply
pipe leading out from the boiler, with 1-inch
returns under the benches, making a satisfactory
system for the lean-to type described in detail
in the previous chapter.

work be nearer than six inches to it. Very small
houses, especially if not started up until January,
may be heated by an ordinary wood stove with the
stove pipe run the length of the house, but such an
arrangement will give off a very drying and uneven
heat, and require a lot of attention, to say nothing
of its danger.

By far the most satisfactory way will be to use
hot water. If the size of the house will not justify
the purchase of a small heater — a second-hand
one may often be had at a very reasonable figure —
a substitute may be had by inserting a hot-water coil
in a stove or in the house furnace. In one

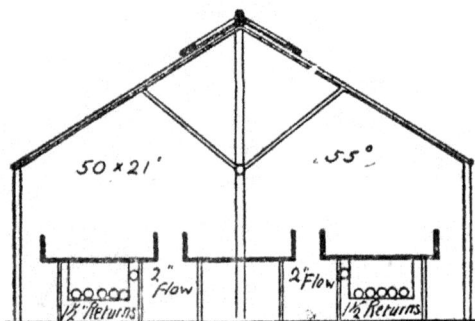

Fig. 9—For the larger greenhouse of the
isolated double-slope type, 21 x 50 feet in size, a
2-inch supply pipe, with five 1½-inch returns
under the outer benches, will secure a temperature of 55 degrees.

of the diagrams is shown an arrangement of
pipes for heating a house 21 x 50 feet, and
in another piping for lean-to described in
the preceding chapter. With the small pipe sufficient for such a house as that illustrated in the latter diagram, the work can be done by anyone at all
acquainted with the use of pipe tools; if possible,
the pipes should be given a slight downward slope,

say one inch in ten feet, from as near the heater as practical. For all this work second-hand piping, newly threaded, will answer very well, and it may be bought for about four cents per foot for one-inch pipe; six cents for one and one-half inch, and eight cents for two-inch. In putting the stove or heater in place, it should be sunk below the level upon which the pipes will run, and attention should also be given to the matter of caring for the fire, removing ashes, etc., making the management of these things as convenient as possible.

CHAPTER XXIII

MANAGEMENT

EXPERIENCE only can teach the beginner just how to manage his vegetables and plants in this new winter garden. But at the outset he must remember one thing: If it is true that he has control of his miniature world of growing things it is also true that he can leave nothing, as he does with his outside garden, to the treatment of nature. The control is in his hands — the warmth, the moisture, the fresh air, the soil — none can be left to chance; he must think of them all. And before going into details, which might at first be confusing, let us take up the elements of this little world over which we are to reign, and try to elucidate first a few general rules to guide us. The house, after countless little delays and unforeseen problems conquered by personal interest and ingenuity, is at last ready, and the bare board benches look ugly enough in the bright, hot sunlight. How are they to be converted into a small Garden of Eden, when all outdoors is chained in the silent desolation of drifted snow? Here is a new task. No longer Nature's assistant, the gardener has been given entire management of this new sort of garden. It is

almost a factory, where he must take his raw materials — earth, water, heat, light, and the wonderful thread of life, and mold these all into a hundred marvelous forms of beauty and utility. Something of art, something of science, something of
business, must all be brought to his interesting work.

Let us begin then at the bottom. What is the
best kind of dirt to use? It should be friable, so
that it will not bake and cake in the pots; rich, that
the little plants may readily find ample nourishment;
porous, that water may be soaked up readily, and
any surplus drained off freely. A soil answering
all these requirements is made as follows: cut from
an old ditch or fence-side, thick sods, and stack them
with the grass sides together to rot. This heap
should be forked over several times, when it has
begun to decompose. In dry weather, if within
reach of the hose, a good soaking occasionally will
help the process along. The sods should be cut
during spring or summer. To this pile of sod,
when well rotted (or at time of using), add one-
third in bulk of *thoroughly rotted manure* — cow
and horse mixed, and a year old, if it can be obtained — and mix thoroughly. If the soil is clayey
or heavy, add enough coarse sand and make it fine
and friable, or use a larger proportion of the
manure. Leaf-mould, from the woods, will also be
good to lighten it with. This one mixture will do
for all your potting. Keep enough of it under

cover, or where it will not freeze, to last you during
the winter and early spring. Store some of it in
old barrels, or in boxes under the greenhouse bench,
if there is not a more convenient place. For very
small pots, run it through a half-inch sieve. For
the larger sizes, three inches and up, this will not
be necessary — just be sure the ingredients are
well mixed.

Proper temperature is more likely to be the beginner's stumbling block than any other one thing.
Different plants, of course, require different treatment in this respect; and just as your corn and
beans will not come up if planted too early in the
spring, or carrot or pansy seed in the heat of July,
so the temperature in which a coleus will thrive
would be fatal to the success of verbenas or lettuce
under glass. It will often pay, where a variety
of things are to be grown in the small greenhouse,
to have a glass partition separating it into two sections, one of which may be kept, either by additional
piping or less ventilation, several degrees warmer
than the other. So, while a general collection of
many plants can be grown successfully in the same
temperature, it is foolish to try everything Only
actual experiment can show the operator just what
he can and cannot do with his small house. Even
where no glass partition is used, there will probably
be some variation in temperature in different parts
of the house, and this condition may be turned to

advantage.   The beginner, however, is more likely
to keep his house too hot than too cool. He may
seem at first to be getting a fine quick growth, and
then wonders why things begin to be lanky, and
yellow, forgetting that his plants can get no air to
breathe, except what he is careful enough to give
to them.   For the majority of those plants which the
beginner is likely to try — geraniums, petunias,
begonias, fuchsias, abutilon, heliotrope, ferns, etc.,
a night temperature of 45 to 55 degrees, with 10 to
20 degrees higher during the day, will keep them in
good growing condition during the winter, providing they are neglected in no other respect.   So
long as they are not chilled, they cannot have too
much fresh air during sunny days.   Make it your
aim to keep the temperature as *steady* as possible —
the damage done to plants is as often the result of
sudden changes in temperature as of too high or too
low a temperature.

If it is easy to overdo in the matter of temperature, it is even more so in watering.   A soil such
as described above, when watered, will absorb the
water rapidly, and leave none of it standing upon
the surface of the pots after a few moments.   Practice, and practice only, can teach just when the soil
has been sufficiently saturated.   It should be watered until wet clear through, but never until it
becomes muddy.   And when watered it should not
be watered again until dry — not baked and hard,

but a condition indicated by a whitening of the surface, and the rapidity with which it will again soak up water, a condition hard to describe exactly, but at once recognizable after a little practice. During the dull winter months, it will be sufficient for most plants in the greenhouse to receive water twice a week, or even less often, but on the coming of warm spring days, more frequently, until care is needed daily. There are some old fogy ideas about soft and tepid water, which may help confuse the beginner: they accomplish nothing more. Recent experiments, made by one of the State experiment stations, have confirmed the experience of practical florists, that the temperature of water used, even to ice water, has almost absolutely no effect — the reason being that the water applied changes to the temperature of the soil almost before it can reach the roots of the plant at all. And hard and soft, spring and cistern water, have likewise been used without difference in results. The main thing is to attend to your watering regularly, never letting the plants get dried out or baked.

Not the least important of the " arts " which the worker under glass has to acquire is that of potting. From the time the cuttings in the sand bench are rooted, until the plants are ready to go outdoors in the spring, they have to be potted and repotted. The operation is a very simple one when once acquired. To begin with the cutting: Take a two-

inch pot (a few of the geranium cuttings may require a 2 1-2 inch pot), fill it level with the sifted
soil and with the forefinger make a hole large enough
to receive the roots of the cutting and half its length,
without bending the roots up. With the thumbs
press down the dirt firmly on either side of the
cutting, and give the pot a clean, short rap, either
with the hand or by striking its bottom against the
bench (which should be about waist-high) to firm
and level the earth in it. With a little practice this
operation becomes a very easy and quick one. Place
the pots side by side and give a thorough watering.
Keep in a shaded place, or shade with newspapers,
for four or six days, and as soon as growth begins,
move the pots apart, to allow the free circulation of
air before the plants crowd. The time for repotting in a larger size pot is shown by the condition
of the roots; they should have formed a network
about the side of the pot, but not have remained
there long enough to become tough or hard. They
should still be white " working " roots. To repot,
remove the ball of earth from the old pot, by inverting, striking the rim of the pot against the edge of
the bench (a light tap should be sufficient), taking
care to have the index and middle finger on either
side of the plant stem, to hold it readily. Put in
the bottom of the new pot sufficient earth to bring
the top of the ball of roots, when placed
upon it, a little below the rim of the pot. Hold

this ball firmly in the center of the new pot, and fill
in the space about it with fresh earth, packing it in
firmly, using either the fingers or a bit of wood of
convenient size. As a usual thing it is best when
shifting to use a pot only one size larger. For pots
above four inches in diameter, provide drainage by
" crocking." This is accomplished by putting irregular shaped bits of stone, charcoal, cinders or
pieces of broken pots in the bottom, being careful
not to cover or plug up the hole.

If the pots are placed directly on the bottom of
the bench — board, slate, tile or whatever it is —
they will dry out so quickly that it is next to impossible to keep them properly watered. To overcome this difficulty, an inch or two of sand, or two
or three inches of earth, is placed on the benches.
When placing the pots upon this covering, work
them down into it, just a little, instead of setting
them loosely on top of it.

There are several insect pests which are likely
to prove quite troublesome if given a start and the
proper conditions in which to develop — crowded
plants, too much heat, lack of ventilation, too little
moisture. Prevention is the best cure. Burn tobacco stems or tobacco dust, used according to directions, every week (or oftener if required), and
see that no bugs appear. One or two of the strong-
est brands of tobacco dust for sprinkling are also
used successfully applied directly to the insects *on*

the plants, but my experience with most of these has proved them next to worthless. (See also Chapter XVII.)

It is not nearly so interesting to read about the various greenhouse operations as it is to *do them.* It is work of an entrancing nature, and no one who had never taken a little slip of some new or rare plant and nursed it through the cutting stage and watched its growth till the first bud opened, can have an idea of the pleasure to be had. In the next chapter I shall attempt to explain just how to handle some of the most satisfactory flowers and vege-tables, but the inexperienced owner of a small greenhouse who wishes to make rapid progress should *practice* with every plant and seed that comes his, or her, way, until all the ordinary operations have become as easy as falling off a street car with him. Mistakes will be made, and disappointments occur, of course, but only through these can skill and efficiency be obtained.

CHAPTER XXIV

THERE are a number of greenhouse crops which are easily within the reach of the amateur who has at his disposal a small glass structure. One is apt to feel that something much more elaborate than the simple means at his hands are required to produce the handsome flowers or beautiful ferns which may be seen in the florist's window. It is true that many things are beyond his achievement. He cannot grow gigantic American Beauties on stems several feet long, nor present his friends at Christmas with the most delicate orchids; but he can very easily have carnations more beautiful, because they will be fresher if not quite so large, than any which can be had at the glass-fronted shops; and cyclamen as beautiful, and much more serviceable, than any orchid that ever hung from a precarious basket. To accomplish such results requires not so much elaborate equipment as unremitting care — and not eternal fussing but regular thought and attention.

There is, for instance, no more well beloved flower than the carnation, which entirely deserves the place it has won in flower-lovers' hearts beside, if not

actually ahead of, the rose.   As a plant it will stand
all kinds of abuse, and yet, under the care which
any amateur can give it, will produce an abundance
of most beautiful bloom.   Within a comparatively
few years the carnation, as indeed a number of other
flowers, has been developed to nearly twice its
former size, and the number of beautiful shades
obtainable has also increased many times.

To be grown at its best the carnation should have
a rather cool temperature and plenty of ventilation,
and these two requirements help to place it within
reach of the small greenhouse operator.   If only
a few plants are to be grown, they may be purchased
from a local florist, or obtained by mail from a seed
house.   If as few as two or three dozen plants are
to be kept — and a surprising number of blooms
may be had from a single dozen — they may be kept
in pots.   Use five- or six-inch pots and rich earth,
with frequent applications of liquid manure, as described later.   If, however, part of a bench can be
given to them, the results will be more satisfactory.
The bench should be well drained and contain four
or five inches of rich soil, such as already described.
If it is too late to compose a soil of this kind, use
any rich garden loam and well rotted manure, in
the proportions of five or six to one.   For plants
to begin blooming in the early winter, they should
be put in during August, but for one's own use a
later planting will do.   For this year, if you are too

late, get a few plants and keep them in pots. Next year buy before March a hundred or so rooted cuttings, or in April small plants, and set them out before the middle of May. Cultivate well during the summer, being sure to keep all flower buds pinched off, and have a nice supply of your own plants ready for next fall.

In putting the plants into the bench (or pots) select a cloudy day, and then keep them shaded for a few days, with frequent syringing of the foliage, until they become established. Keep the night temperature very little above fifty degrees, and not above seventy-five in the daytime, while sixty will do in cloudy weather. As to the watering, they should be well soaked when put in, and thereafter only as the ground becomes dry, when it should again be wet, care being taken to wet the foliage as little as possible. In the mornings, and on bright days, syringing the foliage will be beneficial, but never in dull weather, as the leaves should never be wet over night.

As the flower stems begin to shoot up they will need support. If you can get one of the many forms of wire supports used by commercial florists, so much the better; but if these are not obtainable the old method of stakes and strings (or preferably raffia) will do very well. To obtain large flowers the flower stems must be " disbudded " — that is all but the end bud on each stalk should be pinched off, thus throwing all the strength into one large flower. If, on the other hand, the terminal bud is taken off, and several of the side buds left, the result will be a beautiful cluster of blooms, more pleasing, to my mind, than the single large flowers, though not so valuable commercially.

There are any number of wonderful new varieties, but the white, pink and light pink Enchantress, and one of the standard reds will give satisfaction.

VIOLETS

Requiring even less heat than the carnation is the old-time and all-time favorite, the violet. With no greenhouse at all, these can be grown beautifully, simply with the aid of a coldframe. But where a house is to be had, the season of blooming is, of course, much longer. The essential thing is to get strong, healthy plants. As with the carnations, if only a few are wanted, they may be grown in pots, using the six-inch size. The soil, whether for pots or benches, should be somewhat heavier than that prepared for carnations, using one-fourth to one-fifth cow manure added to the loam or rotted sod. If a bench is used, select one as near the glass as you can. Take in the plants with as little disturbance as possible, and keep them shaded for a few days, as with carnations. The plants will require to be about eight inches apart. As for care, apply water

only when the bed has begun to dry, and then until
the bench is soaked through. Pots will, of course,
require more frequent attention in this matter than
a bench. Keep all old leaves picked off and the soil
stirred about the plants, with syringing and fumigating as suggested on page 134. The temperature will be best as low as forty-five degrees
at night, and as little above fifteen more in the daytime as possible. Where no artificial heat can be
had, a fine crop through the spring months may be
had by making a smaller frame inside the regular
coldframe, and packing this space with fine dry
manure, as well as banking the outer frame. This
arrangement, with two sash and mats in the coldest
weather, will keep the plants growing most of the
winter, and certainly the abundance of fragrant
blooms at a season when flowers are most scarce will
amply repay you for the trouble. Some prefer the
single to the double blossoms. Marie Louise and
Lady Hume Campbell (double blue); Swanley
White, and California and Princesse de Galles
(single blue) are the best varieties. Plants may be
purchased of most large florists or from seedsmen.

FERNS

Many of the decorative ferns may also be grown
to perfection in the small house, at a moderate
temperature, fifty to sixty degrees, the nearer sixty

the better.   The Boston fern (*Nephrolepis exaltata Bostoniensis*) and its improved form, *Scottii*, are
two of the best for house use, and if grown in the
greenhouse until of good size and form, they will
make unusual and very acceptable holiday or birth-
day gifts.   A few small plants obtained from the
florist and kept where they do not get a direct glare
of light, watered frequently enough so that the soil
is always moist (but never " sopping "), and plenty
of fresh air in bright weather, will rapidly make
fine plants.   If you happen to have a few old
plants on hand, they may be increased readily by division.   Separate the old crowns into a few small
plants.   Don't make them very small or they will
not renew as readily.   Keep them, if possible, a little above sixty degrees, with plenty of moisture.
Loam and sand, to which is added about the same
amount of leaf-mould, will make a proper soil.

Asparagus ferns will also respond to about the
same care, though thriving in an even lower temperature.   *Asparagus plumosus nanus*, the Lace fern,
is especially delicate and graceful and makes an ideal
small table plant to use with flowers.

CHRYSANTHEMUMS

These are propagated by cuttings, which root
very easily.   I would suggest, however, dipping
them first in a wash of one part Aphine to thirty-
five parts water, and then rinsing in clear cold

water, in order to rid them entirely of any black aphis there may be present. Give them a clean start, and it will be much easier to keep them clean, as they must be kept to make good healthy plants.

If you have not already a stock on hand, I would suggest going to some florist's in the chrysanthemum season and making a list of the varieties which particularly please you. Later, say in February or March, you can get cuttings of these, already rooted if you like, but it's more fun to root them yourself.

Pot off in two-and-one-half-inch pots, and shift on as rapidly as the roots develop. Use, after the first potting, a very rich soil, and give plenty of water. Chrysanthemums are very gross feeders and the secret of success with them lies in keeping them growing on from the beginning as rapidly as possible, without a check. Keep at about fifty-five degrees and repot as frequently as required.

If they are to be grown in a bed or bench, have the soil ready by the first part of June. The distance apart will be determined by the method by which they are to be grown — six or eight inches if to "single stems" with the great big flowers one sees at the florist's; about eight, ten or twelve if three blooms are to be had from each plant. Of course that will be determined by individual taste; but personally I prefer the "spray" form, growing a dozen or more to each plant. They should be syringed frequently and given partial shade. A good way is to spray onto the roof a mixture of lime-water, about as thick as milk, or white lead and naphtha in solution.

As soon as they are well established and growing, decision must be made as to how they are to be grown. If more than one flower to a plant is wanted, pinch out the big top bud and as the side buds develop, take them all off to the number of flowers required, two, three or more as the case may be. If sprays are wanted, pinch out the end buds of these side shoots also when they get about three inches long, and all but a few of the side buds on the shoots.

If at any time during growth the plants seem to be checked, or lose their healthy dark green color, it is probable that they are not getting enough food and should be given top dressings or liquid manure accordingly.

Or if one does not want to devote space in the greenhouse to them for so long a time (although they occupy it when there is little other use for it) the plants may be grown in pots, the final shift being into six- or seven-inch. They are kept in a cool house, or in a shaded place out-of-doors, plunged in coal ashes. One advantage of this method is, of course, that they can be brought into the dwelling house while in bloom.

In either case, the plants must be watched carefully for black fly, which can be kept off with

Aphine.   The plants will also need supports of
twine or wire, or stakes, whether in the beds or in
pots.

The usual method is to cut back the plants after
blooming, store in a cold place and start later into
new growth for cuttings.   A better way is to set a
few plants out early in the spring — one of each
variety will give an abundance of plants for home
use.   Cuttings can be taken from these that will be
just right for late flowers.   These stock plants are
cut back in the fall, taken up and stored in a deep
box, keeping as cold as possible without freezing.

Varieties are so numerous, so constantly changing, of so many types, that it would be unsatisfactory to give a list.   The best way, as mentioned before, is to get a list of the sort you like, while they
are in bloom at the florists.

ROSES

It is much more difficult to grow good roses than
to grow either chrysanthemums or carnations.
They are more particular as to soil and as to temperature, and more quickly affected by insects and
disease.

Nevertheless there is no reason why the amateur
who is willing to be painstaking should not succeed
with the hardier varieties.   Some roses are much
more easily grown than others.   Plants may be
grown from cuttings of the ripened wood, which

should have become too hard to comply with the
" snapping test " (see page 30) used for most other
plants.   By far the best way for the beginner, however, is to buy from the nurserymen or florist.   This
is especially true of the many sorts which do better
when grafted on a strong growing stock.

There are two ways of buying the plants: either
in the dormant state, or growing, out of pots.   In
the first way you get the dry roots and canes (2-
year olds) from the nursery as early as possible in
the spring and set them in nine-inch pots to plunge
outdoors, or boxes, allowing 6 x 6 to 12 inches for
room if you want them for use in the house in the
winter.   Cut back one-half at time of planting,
and after watering to bring the soil to the right
degree of moisture, go very light with it until the
plants begin active growth, when it is gradually increased.   As with chrysanthemums, as the plants
get large, fertilizers and liquid manure must be
given to maintain the supply of plant food.   Let
the plants stay out when cold weather comes, until
the leaves have dropped and then store until December or January in a cold dry place where they
will not be frozen too hard or exposed to repeated
thawings — a trial that few plants can survive.
Bring into warmth as required.

The above treatment is for plants for the house.
For the greenhouse bench get plants that are growing.   They should be clean and healthy, in four- or

five-inch pots. They are set 12 x 12 to 12 x 16 inches apart, depending upon whether the variety is a very robust grower. The best time for setting is April to July first, according to season in which it is desired to get most bloom. As a rule early planting is the more satisfactory.

One of the most important points in success with roses is to provide thorough drainage. Even when raised beds are used, as will generally be the case in small houses, wide cracks should be left every six inches or so. If the house is low, room may be saved by making a " solid " bed directly upon the ground, putting in seven or eight inches of prepared soil on top of two or three inches of clinkers, small stone or gravel.

The preparation of the soil is also a matter of great importance. It should be rather " heavy," that is, with considerably more clay than average plant soil. Five parts rotted loam sod, to one to two parts rotted cow manure, is a good mixture. *It should be thoroughly composted and rotted up.* When filling the bench press well down and if possible give time to settle before putting in the plants.

The plants should be set in firmly. Keep shaded and syringe daily in the morning until well established. Great care must be taken to guard against any sudden changes, so that it is best to give ventilation gradually and keep a close watch of temperature, which should be kept from fifty-five to fifty-eight at night in cold weather.

Care should be taken to water early in the morning, that the leaves may dry off by night. At the same time it is well to keep the atmosphere as moist as possible to prevent trouble from the red spider (see page 134) which is perhaps the greatest enemy of the rose under glass.

As large growth is reached, liquid manure or extra food in the form of dry fertilizer must be given, a good mixture for the latter being 1 lb. of nitrate of soda, one of sulphate of potash and ten of fine bone. Wood ashes sprinkled quite thick upon the soil and worked in are also good.

As the plants grow tall, they will have to be given support by tying either to stakes or wires. It is well to pick off the first buds also, so that mature growth may be made before they begin to flower heavily.

The plants should at all times be kept scrupulously clean.

The roses suited for growing in pots or boxes, to be dried off and brought into heat in January or February, are the hybrid perpetuals, and the newer ramblers, Crimson, Baby White and Baby Pink.

For growing in benches, as described, the teas are used. Among the best of the standard sorts of these are Bride, Perle, Kaiserin Augusta Victoria, Bridesmaid, Pres. Carnot, Meteor, Killarney. New sorts are constantly being tried, and some of these are improvements over old sorts. The catalogues give full description.

For growing at a low temperature, fifty-five degrees or so, the following are good: Wootton, Papa Gontier, red; Perle, yellow; Bridesmaid, large pink; Mad. Cousin, small pink; Bride, white. The above will make a good collection for the beginner to try his or her hand with.

CHAPTER XXV

VEGETABLES

WHILE tomatoes and cucumbers require a high temperature, lettuce may be grown easily all the year round. A good method is to grow three crops of lettuce during the fall and winter, and follow with tomatoes and cucumbers in the spring, when the high temperature required can be more easily maintained.

Lettuce is a low-temperature plant, and there is no reason why the small greenhouse owner should not be able with ease to supply his table constantly with this delicious salad. As with the carnations, and violets, if there is no part of a bench that can be devoted to the lettuce, a few plants can be grown in pots. If this method is used, the seedlings should be pricked off into small pots. When these begin to crowd they will have to be given six to eight inches of room, and the pots plunged in soil to their full depth. But it will be more satisfactory to devote a part of a bench, a solid one if possible and in the coldest part of the house, to the lettuce plants. Well rotted manure, either horse or mixed, and a sandy loam, will make the right soil. The first sowing of seed should be made about August first, in a shaded bed out-of-doors; the seedlings transplanted, as with spring lettuce, to flats or another bed. By the last week in September these will be ready to go into the beds prepared for them, setting them about six inches apart for the loose and eight for the heading varieties. The bed should be well drained, so that the soil will never stay soggy after watering. The soil should be kept fairly dry, as too much moisture is apt to cause rot, especially with the heading sorts. Syringe occasionally on the brightest days, in the morning. Keep the surface of the bed stirred until the leaves cover it. Keep the temperature below fifty at night, especially just after planting, and while maturing. And watch sharply for the green aphis, which is the most dangerous insect pest. If tobacco fumigation is used as a preventive, as suggested, they will not put in an appearance. The first heads will be ready by Thanksgiving, and a succession of plants should be had by making *small* sowings of seed every two or three weeks. If the same bed is used for the new crops, liquid manure, with a little dissolved soda nitrate, will be helpful.

If a night temperature of sixty degrees can be assured in part of the house, tomatoes and cucumbers may also be had all winter. If the house is only a general purpose one, held at a lower temperature than that, they may still be had months before the crop outside by starting them so as to follow

the last crop of lettuce, which should be out of
the way by the first of April. The seeds of either
need a high temperature to germinate well, and
may be started on the return heating pipes, care being taken to remove them before they are injured
by too much shade or by drying out. In sowing the
cucumber seed, pots or small boxes, filled about half-
full of a light sandy compost, may be used, these to
be filled in, leaving only two plants in each, as the
plants get large enough, with a rich compost. If
there is a solid bed available, a trench filled with
horse manure, well packed in, will act as a hotbed
and help out the temperature required for rapid
growth. If fruits are wanted for the winter, the
tomatoes should be started in July and the cucumbers early in August. They should be given a very
rich and sandy soil, and the day temperature may
run up to eighty degrees. Until the latter part of
spring, when the ventilators are opened and bees
have ready access, it is necessary to use artificial
fertilization in order to get the fruit to set. With
a small soft brush, dust the pollen over the pistils.
With the English forcing cucumbers, this will not
be necessary. While fruit is setting, the houses
should be kept especially dry and warm.

The vines of both tomatoes and cucumbers will
have to be tied up to stakes or wires with raffia.
They should be pinched off at about six feet, and,
for the best fruit, all suckers kept off the tomatoes.

The best varieties of tomatoes for forcing are Lorillard, Stirling Castle and Comet; of the cucumbers, Arlington White Spine, Davis Perfected and the English forcing varieties.

If you do not like to stop having lettuce in time to give up space to cucumbers or tomatoes, start some plants about January first, and have a hotbed ready to receive them from the flats before March first. With a little care as to ventilation and watering, they will come along just after the last of the greenhouse crops.

A point not to be overlooked in connection with all the above suggestions is that any surplus of these fresh out-of-season things may be disposed of among your vegetable-hungry friends at the same step-ladder prices they are paying the butcher or green-grocer for wilted, shipped-about products.

And don't get discouraged if some of your experiments do not succeed the first time. Keep on planning, studying and *practicing* until you are getting the maximum returns and pleasure from your glass house.

Tomato plants, started in pots, ready for transplanting into the bench

The tomato plants in full bearing. The vines are severely pruned and tied up to sticks or twine

Lettuce and cucumbers in the greenhouse. The cucumber vines are induced to climb the heavy strings so as to economize bench space

CHAPTER XXVI

VEGETABLE AND BEDDING PLANTS FOR SPRING

WHILE it is true that there are many ways in which one may save money with a small greenhouse all through the year, the best chance for making money is by growing vegetable and bedding plants in the spring. Bedding stock is what the florists term geraniums, coleus, begonias and other plants used for setting out flower beds in the spring.

In every community a large number of such plants are used and the case will be rare indeed in which one will meet with any difficulty in disposing of quite a number of such plants among immediate neighbors and friends.

The number of plants which can be grown in the spring with even a very small house and a few sash is quite surprising. The secret of the mystery lies, of course, in the fact that in their early stages, seedlings and cuttings, the plants occupy very little room; while as soon or soon after they are transplanted or shifted to large pots they are shoved outdoors into coldframes. 'As the tender vegetables, such as tomatoes, peppers, egg-plant, etc., are not started until after the hardier ones, cabbage, lettuce, cauliflower,

etc., the frames can be filled up again usually as fast
as emptied. In the same way heliotrope, salvia,
coleus and other tender plants follow pansies,
daisies, carnations, etc.

It will thus be seen that to grow these plants to
the best advantage, a coldframe, or better still, both
a coldframe and hotbed, will be used in conjunction
with the small home greenhouse.

Directions have already been given (see Chapter
IV) in these pages for sowing, starting and transplanting seed.

VEGETABLES

The dates for sowing are about as follows in the
vicinity of New York. Allow about a week's difference for every hundred miles of latitude —
earlier in the south, later in the north.

February 1st—Cabbage, cauliflower.

February 15th—Cabbage, cauliflower, Brussels
sprouts, beets, lettuce, onions for plants.

March 1st — Lettuce, celery (early), tomato
(early), beets.

March 15th — Lettuce, tomato (main), egg-
plant, pepper. For one's own use or special orders,
cucumbers, squash, lima beans, potatoes sprouted
in flats of sand, may also be started, but there is no
market demand for them.

April 1st—Celery (late), cauliflower; (in sods or
paper pots), muskmelon, watermelon, corn, for
special use.

After being started and pricked off into flats,
cabbage, cauliflower, Brussels sprouts, beets, lettuce,
and celery are kept inside just long enough to get
well established, and then put outside in a tight
frame.   Harden off as well as possible before putting out, as a freeze the first night might injure
them.   After that slight frost on the leaves will not
injure them, but if they freeze stiff, apply cold
water in the morning — ice-cold is just as good —
and shade until they are thawed out.   If very cold
it will be necessary to protect the frames with shut-
ters.   Beets and lettuce will not stand quite so low
a temperature as the cabbage group.   By the time
the plants are pretty well grown, cloth-covered
frames may be substituted for the glass ones, and
these may be used elsewhere to cover the tenderer
plants such as tomato and egg-plant.   After the
first of April they will not need any protection.
Last spring I had several thousand cabbages covered
twice with several inches of snow, and hardly a one
was lost.

Tomatoes, peppers and egg-plants require different treatment.   They are heat-loving plants, and
not only succumb to even a slight freeze, but will
be so checked by a low temperature, even if not
touched by frost, that they will amount to little.
They should be kept growing as rapidly as possible.
They will also require a *second* transplanting.
Those wanted for the retail trade are put a dozen

in a box, three or four inches deep and 7 x 9 inches. Care must be taken not to let these plants run up tall. Always give all the air possible while keeping up the temperature, which should be from fifty to fifty-five at night. Get them outdoors as soon as the weather becomes settled, where they could be protected in case of a sudden late frost.

BEDDING PLANTS

Most of the plants used for flower gardens and lawn beds come under the three following classes: (1) Those grown from seed; (2) those grown from cuttings; (3) those of a bulbous nature.

Almost all of the first group are sown in the spring in flats in the greenhouse. Two important exceptions, however, are pansies and English daisies *(Bellis perennis)*. They are sown early in the fall, as already described, and the plants wintered over in a frame or protected outdoors. For the retail trade they are put up in small boxes or " pansy baskets " made for the purpose. While small plants, just beginning to bloom, are the best, it seems very hard to convince a customer of it and they will often choose a basket with four or five old plants loaded with bloom in preference to a dozen small ones.

Asters, alyssum, balsams, candytuft, celosia, coleus, dianthus (pink), lobelia, mignonette, petunias, phlox, portulaca, ricinus, salvia, verbenas, vinca, roses, zinnias, may all be started from seed. The greatest scret of success is to keep the plants from crowding, and keep pinched back to make bushy plants. Salvias and coleus are the tenderest of these plants. The others can go out to the frames, if room is scarce, as soon as the weather becomes settled.

PLANTS FROM CUTTINGS

The method of choosing and rooting cuttings has been outlined in a previous chapter (see page 29). In greenhouse work the main difference is that they are taken in much larger quantities. For this reason it is usually convenient to have a cutting bench instead of the flats or saucers used in rooting house plants. The bench should be three or four inches deep, filled with medium coarse, gritty sand, or a substratum of drainage material. If possible, have it so arranged that bottom heat may be given — this being most conveniently furnished with pipes under the bench boxed in. (The temperature required for most cuttings will be fifty to fifty-five in the house with five to ten degrees more *under* the bench.) The cutting bench should also be so situated that it readily may be shaded, as one of the most important factors of success is to prevent the cuttings from wilting at any time — especially just after placing in the sand. After rooting, the cuttings are put into small pots or flats as already explained.

202 GARDENING INDOORS AND UNDER GLASS

Spring stock of some plants, such as geraniums, are rooted in the fall — September to November. Others, which make a quick growth, such as petunias, not until early in the spring,— last of January to April, but for the most part in February. In the former case, cuttings are taken just before frost from outside plants, or later from stock plants lifted and taken indoors; in the latter case, stock plants are taken in and carried through the winter in a more or less dormant or resting condition; being kept rather dry and started into active growth in January. The new growth furnishes material for cuttings, which are grown on as rapidly as possible.

The following plants are treated in one of the above ways; further details in any case may be found in the first part of the book:

Alternantheres	Heliotrope
Begonias, fibrous rooted	Ice Plant
Coleus	Paris Daisy
Cuphia	Petunias
Geraniums	Salvias
Ivy Geraniums	Vincas

German Ivy

BULBOUS BEDDING PLANTS

The bulbous plants are started directly in pots, or in flats and transferred to pots, as described in individual cases in the preceding pages.

Cannas, tall   Caladiums
Cannas, dwarf flowering Tuberous rooted
Dahlias   Begonias
are the sorts for which there is most demand.

CONCLUSION

Condensed as the latter part of this book has had
to be, I trust it may give the reader a glimpse of the
pleasure, and even of the possibility for profit, that
is offered by the small home glass house.

Do not feel that because you cannot have a large
greenhouse, with all the modern equipment, that it
is not worth while to have any. Many of the large
establishments in the country have grown from just
such small beginnings as have been described or suggested here.

Possibly you would never be interested in the
commercial side of your under-glass gardening,
even though success crowned your efforts. There
is not, however, any question about the fun and
healthy pleasure to be had, and I can wish you no
more gardening joy than that the coming year will
find you with at least a modest amount of " home
glass."

THE END

INDEX

INDEX

A

Abutilon, 72.
Acalypha, 73.
Accessories, 140.
Achyranthes, 81.
African Blue Lily, 123.
Ageratum, 66.
Alternanthera, 82.
Alyssum, 66.
Amaryllis, 122.
Anemone, 126.
Anthericum, 82.
Aphis, 133.
Araucaria, 82.
Aralia, 73.
Ardisia, 73.
Aspidistra, 83.
Aucuba, 73.
Azalea, 74.

B

Bay-window, 3, 9.
Balsam, 66.
Bedding plants—grown for spring, 200.
Begonia Rex, 53.
Begonias, flowering, 51.
Blood Flower, 124.
Bone meal, 141.
Bouvardia, 74.
Browallia, 75.
Bulbs, Dutch or Cape, 117.
Bulbs, for winter bloom, 116.

C

Cacti, 110.

Caladium, 83, 125.
Calla, 121.
Candytuft, 66.
Carnations, 66, 180.
Cannas, 66.
Chinese Sacred Lily, 127.
Chrysanthemum, 67, 185.
Cissus, 90.
Clematis, 90.
Cobœa Scandens, 91.
Coldframe, 149.
Coleus, 84.
"Crocking" pots, 178.
Cuttings, preparation of, 29.
Cuttings, propagation of, 30.
Cucumbers, 194.

D

Daphne, 75.
Disbudding, 182.
Diseases, 137.
Dracæna, 84.

E

Easter lily, 120.
English ivy, 92.

F

Farfugium, 84.
Ferns, 97, 184.
Fertilizers, 19, 145.
Flowering maple, 72.
Foliage plants, 81.
    Achyranthes, 81.
    Alternanthera, 82.
    Anthericum, 82.
    Araucaria, 82.

Foliage plants (Continued)
  Aspidistra, 83.
  Caladium, 83.
  Cissus, 90.
  Clematis, 90.
  Cobœa scandens, 91.
  Coleus, 84.
  Dracæna, 84.
  English ivy, 92.
  Farfugium, 84.
  German ivy, 92.
  Hoya Carnosa, 91.
  Ivy, 92.
  Leopard plant, 84.
  "Little Pickles," 94, 115.
  Manettia, 93.
  Moneywort, 93.
  Morning-glory, 93.
  Musk plant, 93.
  Nasturtium, 94.
  Othonna, 94.
  Pandanus, 85.
  Pepper, 85.
  Rubber plant, 86.
  Saxifraga, 87.
  Sensitive plant, 88.
  Smilax, 94.
  Sweet peas, 95.
  Thunbergia, 95.
  Tradescantia, 88.
  Vines, 90.
  Zebra plant, 88.
Frozen plants, treatment of,
  199.

G

Genista, 75.
Geranium, 56.
German ivy, 92.
Gladiolus, 124.
Greenhouse, construction of,
  156.
Greenhouse, management of,
  172.
Grevillea, 75.

H

Hanging baskets, 130, 143.
Heating apparatus, 3.
Heating of greenhouses, 167.
Heliotrope, 61.
Hibiscus, 75.
Hotbed, 149.
House plants, 44.
Hoya Carnosa, 91.
Hydrangea, 76.
Hyacinths, 118.

I

Insects, 132.
Insect diseases, remedies for,
  138.
Iris, 126.
Ivy, 92.

K

Kerosene emulsion, 139.

L

Lantana, 77.
Leaf-mould, 141.
Lemon, 77.
Lemon verbena, 77.
Leopard plant, 84.
Lettuce, 193.
Lily-of-the-valley, 125.
Light, proper amount of, 6.
"Little Pickles," 94, 115.
Lobelia, 68.

M

Mahernia (honey-bell), 68.
Manettia, 93.
Manures, 17, 145.
Manure, liquid, 48, 145.
Marguerite carnation, 66.
Mealy bug, 135.
Mignonette, 68.

Moisture, amount of for plants indoors, 12.
Moneywort, 93.
Morning-glory, 93.
Musk plant, 93.

N

Narcissi, 118.
Nasturtium, 94.
Nitrate of soda, 20.
Nitrogen, forms of, 18.

O

Oleander, 77.
Orange, 78.
Othonna, 94.
Oxalis, 120.

P

Palms, 103.
Pandanus, 85.
Pansy, 68, 200.
Patience plant (*impatiens*), 67.
Peat, 141.
Pepper, 85.
Petunia, 62.
Phosphoric acid, forms of, 18.
Pots, 143.
Potting, 38, 176.
Potash, forms of, 18.
"Plunging" pots in summer, 49.
Primroses (*Primua*), 63.
Propagation, from cuttings, 30.
Propagation, from seed, 22-27.
Propagation, "saucer system," 32.

R

Ranunculus, 126.
Red spider, 134.

Reinwardtia, 78.
Repotting, 40.
Resting periods of plants, 47.
Rex, Begonia, 53.
Root aphis, 136.
Roses, 78, 188.
Rubber plant, 86.

S

Salvia, 68.
Sash, lean-to, 164.
Saxifraga, 87.
Scale, 136.
Sensitive plant, 88.
Shelf, for plants, 8.
Shrubs.
  Abutilon, 72.
  Acalypha, 73.
  Aralia, 73.
  Ardisia, 73.
  Aucuba, 73.
  Azalea, 74.
  Bouvardia, 74.
  Browallia, 75.
  Daphne, 75.
  Flowering maple, 72.
  Genista, 75.
  Grevilla, 75.
  Hibiscus, 75.
  Hydrangea, 76.
  Lantana, 77.
  Lemon, 77.
  Lemon verbena, 77.
  Oleander, 77.
  Orange, 78.
  Reinwardtia, 78.
  Roses, 78-188.
  Swainsona, 79.
  Sweet olive, 79.
Slips, preparation of, 29.
Smilax, 94.
Snapdragon, 64.
Soil, ingredients, 141.
Soil, for greenhouses, 173.
Soil, for pots and boxes, 14.

Sphagnum moss, 141.
Spirea, 126.
Steria, 68.
Stocks, 69.
Sub-watering, 24, 142.
Swainsona, 79.
Sweet olive, 79.
Sweet peas, 95.

T

Temperature, for plants, indoors, 11, 45.
Temperature, for greenhouses, 174.
Thrips, 136.
Thunbergia, 95.
Tomatoes, 194.
Tradescantia, 88.
Transplanting, 35.
Tuberous begonia, 124.
Tulips, 118.

V

Vallota, 123.
Vases, 129.
Vegetable plants, started under glass, 197.
Veranda boxes, 128.
Verbena, 69.
Verbena, Lemon, 77.
Vines, 90.
Violets, 183.

W

Watering, 45.
Watering, for greenhouse, 175.
Window-boxes, 128.
Window-box, construction of, 9-10.
Worms, 137.

Z

Zebra plant, 88.

www.ingramcontent.com/pod-product-compliance
Lightning Source LLC
Chambersburg PA
CBHW060749100426
42813CB00004B/751